I See Him, but Not Now
A Biblical Theology of
Numbers 22-24

Michael Dietzel

ISBN: 1535203803
ISBN-13: 978-1535203807

To Joe Pieri and Josh Pruden, my fellow pioneers who provided needed exhortation and encouragement as we wrote our theses together.

To Dr. André Gazal, our fearless leader who provided faithful guidance and direction as he oversaw our writing.

Michael Dietzel

Table of Contents

Michael Dietzel

Preface

The origins of this book trace back to January 2014. While taking a graduate level class at Northland International University on biblical theology called the Story of Scripture taught by Jim Hamilton and Matthew Harmon, I received the assignment of writing a short paper in the realm of biblical theology. I chose to study Numbers 22-24 and the story of Balaam as it had been mentioned in class and peaked my interest. I thoroughly enjoyed the paper and began to focus further on biblical theology as a discipline throughout my studies for a Master's degree.

In January of 2015, I and two other students embarked on our final graduate assignment, a thesis paper on the subject of our choice. Remembering the enjoyable experience I had found with my study of Balaam, I decided to explore the chapters further, moving from a 15 page paper to a 90 page mini book. I wrote it after the style of the New Studies in Biblical Theology series, specifically following the pattern laid out by Jim Hamilton in his work *With the Clouds of Heaven*,[1] a biblical theology of Daniel.

In June of 2016, my close friend and pastor Michael Summers spoke with me concerning the book he had just published, *Surrender: A Christian's Guide to Dependence*,[2] and I was struck with the possibility of publishing my own work. For reasons unknown to me Don Carson and the people behind NSBT had decided not to pick it up as the next work in their series, so I decided to give self-publishing a go.

Given the academic nature of the thesis, I hadn't sought to profligate it among my friends, though I had used the ideas and truths which I gleaned from my study in lessons and conversations. With the encouragement of Michael Summers, I set out to convert the academic thesis to a short, readable explanation of the biblical theological themes in Numbers 22-24. You are reading the result.

I hope this work will accomplish several goals. First, I hope it can serve as an introduction to the realm of biblical theology for those who have never interacted with the discipline. Biblical theology has changed the way I read the Bible and has helped me understand the truth of Scripture with more clarity. If God can use this work to bring that same magnification of clarity to your own study of Scripture, I will be thrilled. Second, I want to highlight God's faithfulness in his interaction with his people.

The story of Balaam glorifies God for his faithfulness, and I want that glory to be seen more clearly. Third, I wish to highlight the preeminence of Jesus' work of salvation and restoration in all of Scripture, even a passage that focuses on a confused magician, an angry king, and a talking donkey.

If anyone finds benefit from this work, I trust that it comes from God speaking through his text, not Michael Dietzel speaking from his own thoughts. I desire to merely say what God has said, and any positive impact it might have on the reader comes from the author of the story, not the 21st century commentator.

A note before the exposition begins: while the content of this work pertains significantly to the discussion of covenant theology and dispensationalism, the scope keeps me from interacting with and discussing the full measure of the conversation. In discussions of how different parts of the story are fulfilled I mean that the fulfillment is certainly found in the interpretation I present and cannot be less than that, but the fulfillment could also be more than that. I intend the observations in the following pages to add to the conversation but not necessarily present final conclusions.

Several people deserve recognition for their help in the completion of this work. Dr. André Gazal supervised Joseph Pieri, Josh Pruden, and myself as we wrote our Masters Theses. Dr. Gazal encouraged me to pursue this topic and provided invaluable input during the writing process. He was also the first person to ever read the completed work. I would have never completed this without the encouragement and perseverance of Joe and Josh as they completed their own theses.

Numerous people at Northland and Countryside deserve recognition for the support they provided in the forms of asking about the progress of my thesis as well. Thank you to all who intentionally or inadvertently pushed me along in the process.

Thank you to Michael Summers for helping me learn the Amazon self-publishing system and always being available to answer my many questions. You were the one who put this idea in my head and followed up to see how I was doing.

Thank you to my mom, Cindy Dietzel, for serving as my editor and giving me large amounts of detailed feedback. You were the one who taught me to read and write, who taught me proper grammar and writing skills. This book is the result of all your hard work.

Philip Palmer painted the beautiful cover of this book and I am deeply indebted to him. He skillfully portrayed the beauty of Numbers 22-24 in a visually stunning way of which I am incapable. Kelly Buss turned the raw beauty of that image and turned into a polished final product. I'm thankful to them both for their incredible skills in areas in which I lack.

Finally, Dr. Chris Bruno and Dr. Jonathan Arnold were kind enough to take time to read my manuscript and provide feedback from the perspective of an already published theological author. I took graduate level classes from them at

Northland and I'm grateful for their discipleship in my life from that time in school until now in this endeavor.

It takes a village to write a book, and I'm thankful for all the help and support I've received in making this a reality.

Now then, let's talk about magicians, donkeys, and biblical theology.

Michael Dietzel

Part 1: Preliminary Questions

Michael Dietzel

Chapter 1

What is Biblical Theology?

The subtitle of this book identifies it as a biblical theology of Numbers 22-24. What does it mean that it is a biblical theology? Isn't all theology biblical? Technically theology (the study of God) is biblical (coming from God's Word) because what we know from God is what he has revealed of himself to us in his Word. But the concept of biblical theology cannot be defined by merely looking at the etymology of the words "biblical" and "theology." It is more than theology that is derived from the Bible.

Biblical theology is the name given to a certain way of

doing theology. It is a specific style of studying and interpreting the Bible. It is not the only way to do theology, but it serves as one of many helpful tools in studying God's Word. Other tools include systematic theology, historical theology, apologetics, hermeneutics, and biblical languages.

Biblical theology has come into greater focus during the last century and a half, and many current authors are providing key insights into the discipline. As the concept has become more popular, many have provided definitions and descriptions of what biblical theology means. James Hamilton defines biblical theology as "the attempt to understand and embrace the interpretive perspective of the biblical authors."[1] This means that those who do biblical theology seek to read the Bible in the way the authors themselves read the Bible. We should look to see how Paul interpreted Old Testament passages to understand how we should read them. Stephen Dempster agrees, saying that the goal of biblical theology "is to discover the Bible's distinctive theology."[2]

One of the most important aspects of biblical theology is that of themes. Determining how one scriptural author reads and interprets another is admittedly difficult, and one of the greatest helps is to look for the themes that are employed by multiple authors. Looking for the themes that authors intentionally choose to include and seeing how they develop those themes forms the core of biblical theology.

If you think this sounds similar to systematic theology,

you're right. Both biblical theology and systematic theology focus on themes in Scripture. The difference is in their approach. While systematic theology takes a theme and asks, "What does the Bible say about this theme?," biblical theology looks at the Bible and asks, "What are the themes that the authors repeatedly focus on?" Systematic theology approaches Scripture deductively, biblical theology approaches Scripture inductively. Both provide good and needed input to theological study, and neither one is more right or wrong than the other. They are merely different.

Biblical theology is helpful because it emphasizes what was important to the biblical authors. While systematic theology provides answers to the common questions humans ask when they approach Scripture, biblical theology provides the answers to the common questions the authors asked as they approached Scripture. This allows us to emphasize the things that are truly important in the bible as the authors show us what they deemed important.

So, if biblical theology means seeking to see Scripture the way the biblical writers did, specifically by means of seeing the themes which are repeated through the Bible, we need to know who the authors of Scripture and what themes they include. And if this book is a biblical theology of Numbers 22-24, we need to know who the author of Numbers is and which themes he includes.

That is precisely what the following chapters will explore. We will start by studying who wrote Numbers. Then we will traverse the text of Numbers 22-24 to become familiar with the story and see what themes are prominent. Once certain themes are identified, we will flesh them out in three steps. Step one will be to lay the foundation of how that theme has already been treated in previous Scripture. Step two will be to see how the author of Numbers develops the theme within these three chapters. Step three will be to follow the theme throughout the rest of Scripture and see how it expands the contribution of Numbers 22-24.

In this adventure through the text of Scripture and the mind of the author, I hope you come away with a greater clarity of the text of Numbers 22-24 and with a desire to continue doing biblical theology throughout the rest of Scripture. With our map in place, let's hit the road.

Chapter 2

Who Wrote Numbers 22-24?

Early Interpretation

In order to determine the author of Numbers 22-24, we need to determine the author of the entire book of Numbers. And in order to determine the author of Numbers, we need to consider the books around it. Numbers is the fourth book of the Bible, preceded by Genesis, Exodus, and Leviticus and preceding Deuteronomy. These five books together are called the Pentateuch, a word that means a five part work. Another word used to describe these five books is Torah, the Hebrew word meaning law. These books tell different parts of the same story, and readers generally consider them as five distinct but connected parts making up a unified whole.

Unlike some books of the Bible, the author of the Pentateuch never identifies himself or herself. However, there are clues that allow interpreters to make an educated guess about the author. 2 Chronicles 30:16, Ezra 3:2, and Nehemiah 8:12 all mention the law of Moses, describing the law (i.e. the Torah, the first five books of the Bible) as belonging to Moses or as authored by Moses. 2 Chronicles 25:4 equates the Torah with the book of Moses as well. Several times the Pentateuch records Moses writing, whether events (Exodus 17:14; Numbers 33:2), laws (Exodus 24:4; 34:27-28), or songs (Deuteronomy 31:22).

In the New Testament, Matthew 19:7, 22:24 and Mark 7:10 refer to words of the law as words of Moses. Jesus describes the Pentateuch as the book of Moses in Mark 12:26. He also refers to the Torah simply as Moses in Luke 16:29 and 24:27. In addition, John 1:17 says that the law was given through Moses and John 7:23 references the law of Moses.[1]

Without a doubt, the early interpreters of the Pentateuch attribute it to Moses. Beyond the biblical authors, Jewish and Christian authors after the first century continued to attribute the Pentateuch to Moses.[2]

Modern Interpretation

While the overwhelming majority of commentators throughout history believed that Moses authored the Pentateuch, and by inference Numbers, a new interpretation became popular during the Enlightenment. Around the 17th century, scholars began to focus on the differences they found within the text of the Pentateuch. One of these scholars, Julius Wellhausen, popularized the idea that there were four different authors of the Pentateuch.[3]

This emphasis on the disunity of the Pentateuch and the multiple authors stemmed from the idea that the Pentateuch wasn't factual, but rather a myth pieced together by sources after the fact to provide a history for the nation of Israel. Rather than letting the text speak for itself, liberal scholars such as Wellhausen doubted that the content of Scripture was true and sought to explain it in a way that made sense to their scholastic mindset.

These liberal authors looked to Numbers to provide support to their theory. Specifically, they pointed to Numbers 12:3, which says "Now Moses was a very humble man, more humble than anyone else on the face of the earth." If Moses was so humble, why would he include this verse? Liberal scholars pointed to verses like this in their argument for multiple authors.

The multiple author theory dominated scholarship surrounding the Pentateuch for several hundred years. However, most current scholars have gone away from the theory and agreed more with the single authorship of Moses. It is unnecessary to doubt the legitimacy of what Scripture claims about itself, and modern writers agree.

A Compositional Approach

While the liberal approach that stated there were multiple authors is built on faulty presuppositions, it does legitimately point out some disunities and questions about a single author. Would Moses really write that he was the most humble man in the world? Or did he really record his own death and the aftermath in Deuteronomy 34:1-12?

While the Pentateuch itself as well as the rest of Scripture seems to point to Moses as an author of Genesis through Deuteronomy, these internal factors may point to a later editor as well. An Old Testament scholar named John Sailhamer suggests this in a book called *The Meaning of the Pentateuch.*[4] He suggests two main reasons for this theory:

1. **There are several passages in the Pentateuch which Moses would not likely have included.** Beyond identifying Moses as the most humble man alive and describing his death, Deuteronomy 34:10-12 states that no prophet has ever arisen since him. Unless someone had seen all the prophets, they would not be able to make this claim. Certainly Moses couldn't!

2 **The construction of the Pentateuch as a whole indicates the hand of an editor.** Throughout the Pentateuch, a similar pattern emerges. First a narrative, then a poem , followed by an epilogue. The poem sums up the main point of the narrative and hones in on what the reader should learn from the story. The epilogue then returns to the story and links it to the next.[5]

This tripartite pattern occurs nine different times in the Pentateuch. The texts are outlined in the table below.[6]

Narrative	Poem	Epilogue
Creation (Gen 1-2:22)	Adam's poem (2:23)	Epilogue (2:24)
Fall (Gen 3:1-13)	God's poem (3:14-19)	Epilogue (3:20-24)
Cain (Gen 4:1-22)	Lamech's poem (4:23)	Epilogue (4:24-26)
Genealogy (Gen 5:1-28)	(Other) Lamech's poem (5:29)	Epilogue (5:30-32)
Flood (Gen 6:1-9:24)	Noah's poem (9:25-27)	Epilogue (9:28-29)
Patriarchs (Gen 12-48)	Jacob's poem (49:1-28)	Epilogue (49:29-33)
Exodus (Ex 1-14)	Moses' poem (15:1-18)	Epilogue (15:19-21)
Wilderness (Num 10-21)	Balaam's poems (23:1-24:24)	Epilogue (24:25)
Conquest (Ex-Deut)	Moses' poem (Deut 31:30-33:29)	Epilogue (34)

In each of the nine examples a story is followed by an interpretive poem and an epilogue. The final example includes the entire conquest narrative which is summed up by a massive utterance of Moses and the story of his death. This all points to a master hand intentionally shaping material into the form of the Pentateuch we have today.

I would argue that while Moses was the initial author of the law, a later author put together the current form which we now read in our Bible. This second person can be considered an author rather than merely an editor due to the fact that this second hand is still intentionally shaping the Biblical text in order to communicate the truth of God's Word.[7] The specific work of this second author will be considered as we study Numbers 22-24 together.

This proposal does not undermine the inerrancy of the Bible or the inspiration of the Biblical authors, but rather shows how God worked over the course of many centuries and multiple authors to create the Pentateuch even as he worked over multiple millennia and through a multitude of authors to create what believers today consider the canon.

So who wrote Numbers 22-24? Both Moses and a second author contributed to the intentional shaping of this integral story.

But wait, there's more.

Balaam's Contribution

Biblical theology focuses on the intentional input of the author. In Numbers 22-24, Balaam gives several long and important speeches. Though he is not the author in the sense of writing the biblical text, his voice contributes to the meaning of this text. But how?

The answer to this question lies in understanding the role God plays in the authorship of this narrative. Though Moses initially wrote the narrative, the second author edited and compiled the narrative, and Balaam voices the text within the narrative, God ultimately authored Numbers 22-24. He authored these chapters, as well as all of Scripture, through the process of inspiration, as 2 Timothy 3:16-17 describes: "All Scripture is God-breathed and is useful for teaching, rebuking, correcting, and training in righteousness."

That Scripture is God-breathed can be restated that it is breathed out by God or inspired by God. Though this work cannot develop a full explanation of this doctrine, it is sufficient to say that God sovereignly directed the human writers of Scripture to record precisely what he intended. In this way he can truly be described as an author of Scripture, though his authorship differs from the authorship of the humans. God ultimately controls everything recorded in Scripture, including Numbers 22-24, and the human authors are also truly involved in intentionally shaping the story. The human authors shape their writings by the sovereign hand of the divine author.

And so to answer the question of what Balaam intended to communicate, we must turn to the intentions of the one who spoke through him. While on one level God shaped this narrative by guiding the hands of Moses and the later compiler in the act of inspiration, on another level he also shaped the narrative by not allowing Balaam to speak his own words but instead giving him words to say and speaking through him.

On twelve different occasions Balaam attests to his inability to speak or do anything unless the Lord commands him. On six other occasions God commands him regarding whether he can speak or what he should speak. God gives Balaam a word to say in his first two oracles (23:5; 16) and the Spirit of the Lord comes upon and speaks through Balaam in his last two (24:2; 15-16).[8] Therefore, while Balaam spoke these words, he either spoke only what God told him to or served as the mouth through which the Spirit of God spoke. The meaning Balaam intended is that which God intended. God also worked his desired meaning through Moses and the later compiler. The marks of their handiwork are the focus of the following chapters.

But first, we need to learn more about our main character.

Chapter 3

Who is Balaam?

This chapter focuses on the nature of Balaam's character. Because the material is not clear-cut, this has become one of the most discussed parts of the Balaam Oracles in commentary literature. Given Balaam's contribution as an author of this text, it is important to understand his motives, goals, and character in order to see the effect he has on the meaning of Numbers 22-24. This section will develop a sketch of Balaam from the narrative itself, biblical references, and early Jewish literature.

Description from the Narrative

Numbers 22-24 gives both positive and negative sides to

Balaam. He is portrayed as one who was known worldwide for his magical powers. Balaam was known as a diviner, one who could predict the future and determine the course of action that would be taken by a deity.[9] The use of seven alters and bulls in high places shows that Balaam was a diviner, for these are marks of divination.[10]

The fact that Balaam always reminded Balak that he could say nothing other than what God allowed him to also indicates that his ability was predictive. Divination was not outlawed in Israel, but was even practiced in the use of the Urim and Thummim (Exodus 28:30-35; 1 Samuel 2:28; 14:3; 23:6, 9; 28:6; 30:7) and thus, if Balaam was a diviner, it does not reflect badly upon his character.

Balak, however, wanted a sorcerer, not a diviner.[11] This can be seen from his consistent requests for Balaam to curse Israel. He wanted Balaam to change the will of God, not predict it. Likely Balak's knowledge of Balaam's spiritual powers led him to believe Balaam would be able to do what he requested, though Balaam intended to serve as a diviner. This led to Balak's frustration when Balaam speaks blessings, not curses. But Balaam is only doing what he knows, determining the will of the gods, and the truth God reveals to him about Israel is that they are a blessed nation.

However, this picture is not wholly consistent throughout the Balaam narrative. Numbers 22:21-35 tells the story of Balaam being stopped by an angel on the way to Balak. In 22:22 the reader finds that "God was very angry when he went." However, God has just given Balaam permission to go to Balak. This leads some to believe that Balaam was going with the intention to curse Israel, though just verses before he seemed willing to say only what God allowed him to (22:13, 20).[12]

It is difficult to determine the true character of Balaam from Numbers 22-24 alone. With that in mind, let us continue on to the rest of Scripture's testimony about Balaam.

Later Biblical References to Balaam

Biblical authors explicitly mention Balaam nearly a dozen times after Numbers 22-24. The first passage to refer to him is Numbers 31, where Israel defeats the Midianites in battle. In verse 16 of chapter 31, Balaam is credited with inciting the sexual disaster of Israelite men with Midianite and Moabite women in Numbers 25 which resulted in the death of twenty-four thousand Israelites. Chapter 31 also records that Israel killed Balaam along with the Midianites (31:8). These references are clearly negative towards Balaam, albeit for something he did outside of Numbers 22-24.

Moses also mentions Balaam in Deuteronomy 23:4-6. In speaking to Israel about Moab, he reminds them that Balak sought to curse them through Balaam, but God preserved them by not listening to Balaam. In this reference Balaam is presented as one who sought to curse Israel, though God intervened. Joshua 13:22 mentions Balaam's death much like Numbers 31:8. A similar statement to Deuteronomy 23 occurs in Joshua 24:9-10, where Joshua, instead of Moses, gives Israel the same reminder.

The next reference occurs outside of the Pentateuch in Micah 6:5. The Lord says, "My people, remember what Balak king of Moab plotted and what Balaam son of Beor answered." This indicates that though Balak desired to curse Israel, Balaam resisted and instead blessed the nation. This is the only positive reference to Balaam in the Old Testament, however, for Nehemiah 13:2, the final reference to Balaam in the Old Testament, says that Balaam tried to curse Israel but God intervened.

The three New Testament references to Balaam are very much alike. In 2 Peter 2:15-16 Peter uses Balaam as an example of false teachers. He "loved the wages of wickedness" and "was rebuked for his wrongdoing by a donkey – an animal without speech – who spoke with a human voice and restrained the prophet's madness." Peter characterizes Balaam negatively and shows him as a person of opposition rather than a follower of God. Jude 11 resembles 2 Peter 2:15-16. Balaam is listed along with Cain and Korah as people who model false teachers. Jude characterizes Balaam as someone whose error is linked to his desire for profit.

The last biblical reference to Balaam occurs in Revelation 2:14 in Jesus' letter to the church in Pergamum. He says, "There are some among you who hold to the teaching of Balaam, who taught Balak to entice the Israelites to sin so that they ate food sacrificed to idols and committed sexual immorality." Here Scripture refers to Balaam's acts of inciting the Midianite and Moabite seduction in Numbers 25. But it also alludes to the story of the angel with a flaming sword stopping him on the road in Numbers 22:22-35 Jesus says that if the believers do not repent he will fight against them with the sword in his mouth in Revelation 2:16. Once again Balaam is listed as a representative of false teaching and the charge of inciting Israel to sexual immorality is added to his greed.

Rabbinical material

The extra-biblical Jewish material is mostly negative towards Balaam. Several sources paint a negative picture of Balaam, ranging from claiming that he desired to curse Israel more than Balak and that he was going to do just as Balak asked him to describing him as a sexual pervert and greedy magician. However, a few Jewish sources describe Balaam positively. Two places in the midrash present Balaam as superior even to Moses.[13] This perspective is far outweighed by the negative portrayal, however.

Final Judgment

Determining the character of Balaam is no easy task. While he seems to be presented as someone who desires to say nothing other than what God gives him to say, Scripture also gives indications that he was fueled by money. In addition, though God spoke blessings upon the people of Israel through him, he did incite one of the greatest failures in Israel's history in Numbers 25. Biblical and Jewish testimony is split, though the vast majority is negative.

Who is Balaam? Perhaps the best way to answer this question is to understand the context of the argument. While questions remain about Balaam's motives and desires, the point of the narrative is to show that God will bless his people, even when someone tries to curse them. Whether the desire to curse comes from Balak alone or from Balak and Balaam together is not important. What matters is that Balaam is nothing more than a donkey, a foolish animal, through whom God speaks, and Balak is nothing more than one rebuked by that donkey.

Thus, Balaam should not be considered either wholly good or wholly bad. He is somewhere in between, at times making right decisions and at times making disastrous ones. Balaam is similar to Israel, an imperfect tool in the hands of a perfect God.[14]

Chapter 4

What Does the Story Say?

Before delving into the prevalent themes of Numbers 22-24, we must answer one final question: What actually happens in the narrative? First, the context of Numbers within the entire Pentateuch will be mentioned, followed by a more narrow focus on the context of Numbers itself. After this, the narrative will be unpacked. Finally, special attention will be given to Balaam's four oracles.

While I will try to explain the story well, for best results I recommend you read Numbers 22-24 yourself before finishing this chapter. Biblical theology is best done by reading the text, rereading the text, and reading the text again. Books like this can help, but nothing can replace reading the text for yourself.

Context of the Pentateuch

The Pentateuch is the beginning of the story of the Bible. It also serves as the record of the origin of the world and the nation of Israel. After God creates the world and establishes his greatest creation, man and woman, as his dominion-exercising representatives in Genesis 1-2, Adam and Eve sin against him when they are tempted by the serpent in chapter 3. This creates a rift that serves as one of the driving themes of the Pentateuch and the rest of the Scriptures: the separation of God and humans. God exiles Adam and Eve and casts them from his presence, but not without giving them hope in Genesis 3:15: "And I will put enmity between you and the woman, and between your offspring and hers; he will crush your head, and you will strike his heel."

The theme of a descendant of Eve who would defeat Satan is developed throughout the pages of the Pentateuch. Even in the following chapter of Genesis, Eve evidences hope that her sons would be that seed (4:1, 25). Chapters 6-9 focus on a singular seed, Noah, as God wipes out all population save one family. The genealogies in 5:1-32, 10:1-32, and 11:10-32 each funnel the attention of the reader towards a specific person who stands at the center of the following narrative.[1] The recipient of the attention of the last of these genealogies is a man named Abram. God promises Abram land, blessing, a great name, and that he would become a great nation (Genesis 12:1-3). The idea of blessing is most prominent, as it is mentioned five times in these three verses, culminating in God's promise to "bless those who bless you and curse those who curse you" (12:3). This five-fold mention of blessing contrasts with the five times cursing is mentioned in Genesis 3-11. [2] Throughout the rest of Genesis the focus shifts from Abraham (who has undergone a name change) to his son Isaac, then to Isaac's son Jacob, and lastly from Jacob to his twelve sons, specifically Judah and Joseph. This focus on the seed of Eve emphasizes God's sovereign hand guiding history to bring a savior to fulfill his promise in Genesis 3:15.

In addition to the seed motif, the story of Genesis begins to focus on Abraham and his descendants dwelling in the land God promised to them. Abraham travels to Canaan, the land of promise, and builds altars in Shechem and Bethel, but because the land was owned by others, he is forced to leave (Genesis 12:4-9). [3] Neither his son Isaac nor his grandson Jacob dwells permanently in the land, and through the treachery of eleven of Jacob's sons and a famine, Jacob's entire family ends up in Egypt (Genesis 37-50). There the seventy members of Jacob's family grows to a great multitude and becomes known as the nation of Israel (Exodus 1:5-7), but the Pharaoh of Egypt forces them into slavery (1:8-14). This was not out of God's control, however, for he had promised Abraham in Genesis 15:12-16 that his descendants would serve in a foreign country for four hundred years.

Just as he said, four centuries after Jacob's family came to

Egypt, God raises up Moses to lead them out of Egypt. God tells Moses, "Then say to Pharaoh, 'This is what the Lord says: Israel is my firstborn son, and I told you "Let my son go, so he may worship me." But you refused to let him go; so I will kill your firstborn son' " (Exodus 4:22-23). This is another reminder of the promise of the seed. God brings his son Israel out of Egypt and into the promised land, saving Israel by sending ten plagues upon the Egyptians and leading the people through the waters of the Red Sea in a great act of salvation. God curses those who curse Abraham's descendants.

Outside of Egypt, God meets with Moses as a representative for the people on Mt. Sinai, giving them the law for the peoples' relationship with God and instructions for the building of the tabernacle. God does both of these things so that he could dwell among them. However, before the tabernacle could even be built, before Moses can even return from Mt. Sinai, Israel builds a golden calf and worships it in place of God (Exodus 32). Finally, the book of Leviticus provides further instructions regarding Israel's holiness, describing a sacrificial system that would be used for the sins of the people. If the manifold stories of the transgressions of all humans are any example, this system is desperately needed.

Context of Numbers

It is with this backdrop that the story of the Bible comes to the book of Numbers.[4] The first two chapters describe the numbering and location of the twelve tribes within Israel. In the midst of the desert, the nation of Israel camps with God's presence in the Tabernacle at the center. The image of Israel presented in this way is intentionally reminiscent of the Garden of Eden set amidst an untamed expanse of land outside it and with God's presence with his people inside of it.

Over four hundred years removed from Jacob taking his family of seventy people to Egypt, the nation of Israel now numbers over six hundred thousand, reminding the reader of the promise to Abraham that his descendants would be a nation like the stars of the sky, the dust of the earth, and the sand of the beach: uncountable.[5] As the description of the location of each tribe is given, the tribe of Judah has prominence, having the largest number of family members in the census and encamping at the entrance to the tabernacle, to the direct east of the presence of God. Chapters 3-9 describe the duties of the Levites and instructions for dealing with certain situations that may arise, continuing the theme of holiness dealt with in Leviticus. At the end of chapter 6 God instructs Aaron how to bless the people, focusing on blessing coming from God's presence with and approval of the people. After celebrating the Passover in chapter 9, the Israelites set up the tabernacle. The presence of God in the form of a pillar of cloud in the day and a pillar of fire at night rests upon it. When this pillar of God's presence departs from the tabernacle, the people follow it, showcasing God as their true leader.

Chapter 10 brings about the departure of Israel from Sinai in accordance with the departure of God's presence from the tabernacle. "After the enumeration of the tribes, the divine blessing and the dedication of the altar of sacrifice, the people are led by the divine presence to Canaan (10:11), the land flowing with milk and honey (Numbers 13:27)."[6]

However, this is where the good news stops.

Chapter 11 records two stories of complaints by Israel and judgments from God. Chapter 12 contains the story of Israel's leadership, Aaron and Miriam, rebelling against God's appointed leader Moses, resulting in God's judgment upon them. In chapter 13, at the entrance to God's promised land for Israel, ten of the twelve spies sent to survey the land evidence a lack of faith in God's power by their report about the unconquerable inhabitants of the land. The people rebel again in chapter 14 in response to this, and God judges them first by not allowing anyone from that generation to enter the land (save the two spies who trusted God and advised Israel to go up and take the land) and second by killing the ten faithless spies. Rather than entering into the promised land, the nation of Israel must now spend the next forty years in the desert while the rebellious generation dies off.

Chapters 15-19 are intermixed with instructions for priestly duties and tales of even more rebellions, led by Korah, a prominent Levite, and joined by many other prominent leaders. In chapter 20, even Moses himself shows a lack of faith in God and is not allowed to enter the promised land. The deaths of Merriam

(20:1) and Aaron (20:23-29) remind the reader that the rebellious generation is passing away and being replaced by a new one.

However, this new generation also rebels in chapter 21, but this time God provides a way of salvation from his judgment. The same is true of chapter 25, where again Israel rebels and sins against God, but God provides salvation. A second census in chapter 26 solidifies the presence of a new generation, and chapters 27-36 contain preparations for the new generation to go into the new land.

The story of Numbers brings Israel, the chosen Abrahamic nation with whom God is present, from Sinai to the pinnacle of their journey, the entrance to Canaan. However, after all that God has done for the nation, Israel proves that they are a disobedient nation by consistently rejecting him. Even as the new, untainted generation comes to the forefront, hints of the same sin as their fathers and mothers come to the forefront. It is in the midst of this setting that the reader encounters the story of Balaam.

Narrative

Now that the context has been established, the narrative of Numbers 22-24 can be discussed. While certain themes from the narrative, and specifically Balaam's oracles, are introduced here, they will be expanded later in part 2 as a part of the discussion of the biblical theology of those themes.

Introduction

Numbers 22:1 provides the immediate setting for the story, placing Israel in the plains of Moab along the Jordan River across from Jericho. In chapter 20, Edom denies Israel passage and Israel leaves peacefully. In chapter 21 the Amorites deny Israel passage and Israel destroys them. In chapter 22, a new power comes into view: Moab. As Israel encamps on the plains of Moab, Balak, King of Moab, begins devising a plan to overcome them. He decides to employ the services of Balaam son of Beor, a prominent diviner in the region. Balak's message to Balaam introduces a main theme in the story: "A people has come out of Egypt; they cover the face of the land and have settled next to me. Now come and put a curse on these people, because they are too powerful for me. Perhaps then I will be able to defeat them and drive them out of the land. For I know that whoever you bless is blessed, and whoever you curse is cursed" (22:5-6).

The last phrase recalls Genesis 12:3, in which God promises Abraham (and by extension, his descendants), "I will bless those who bless you and whoever curses you I will curse." With the highest form of political (Balak, King of Moab) and spiritual (Balaam, prominent diviner) opposition, would God bless Israel and protect his nation? Would he halt these attempts and turn the curse back upon Balaam and Balak?[7] Given the negative presentation of Israel, especially in Numbers 11-21, and the introduction of these powerful antagonists, the text seems to set up an opportunity for Israel to be judged and evil to triumph.

However, the first hints at the real outcome of the story occur in Balaam's response to the messengers (22:8-14). Though they came to him with money for his services (22:7), Balaam informs them that he must wait for a message from the Lord before he can make a decision.[8] The Lord comes to Balaam and tells him, "Do not go with them. You must not put a curse on those people, because they are blessed" (22:12). With this response, the reader is reassured that God does indeed intend to honor his promise to Abraham and Israel and to frustrate those who come against his chosen nation.

Balak, however, does not take no for an answer (a trait which will continue throughout the rest of the story) and sends a larger, grander party with the promise of a lucrative paycheck if Balaam will curse Israel (22:15-17). Balaam responds by saying that he could not speak or act against the command the Lord even for all of Balak's riches, but God again comes to him and this time allows him to go with the condition that he do only as the Lord commands him (22:18-20).

Foreshadowing

The story of Balaam's journey to meet Balak (22:22-35) serves as a microcosm and preview of the narrative that follows.[9] As Balaam sets out to go to Balak, God becomes angry with him. He places an angel with a drawn sword on the path, blocking Balaam from continuing his journey. Balaam somehow doesn't see the angel, showing that perhaps he is not as in-tune with the gods as he claims to be. However, his donkey does notice the angel and tries three times to divert Balaam. Unfortunately, Balaam does not recognize what the donkey is doing.

After the donkey lays down under Balaam in a final attempt to divert the diviner from disaster, Balaam begins to beat the animal. As he does this, the Lord opens the mouth of the donkey to speak to Balaam and then opens the eyes of Balaam to see the angel.[10] The angel rebukes Balaam for beating his donkey, telling him that had the beast not done so, the angel would have killed Balaam. Balaam admits his wrongdoing and promises to return home if the Lord desires. However, the angel allows him to continue, as long as he does as the Lord commands.

In an ironic twist, Moses uses the donkey's interaction with Balaam to typify Balaam's interaction with Balak.[11] The donkey, prompted by Balaam to take him along the path, instead follows the direction of God three times by avoiding the angel, irritating Balaam more each time. Balaam, prompted by Balak to curse Israel, instead follows the direction of God and blesses Israel three times, irritating Balak more each time. This typology shows that Balaam, the great pagan sorcerer, is nothing more than a stubborn donkey in the hand of God. As the donkey was unable to do anything of his own volition when faced with the angel of God, so Balaam will be unable to act on his own accord when confronted with the Lord.

The typology leads to implications for Balak as well. While

Balaam, the type, has his foot crushed by the donkey (22:25), Balak, Balaam's antitype, will have his head crushed by the star and scepter of Jacob (24:15). This recalls Genesis 3:15, where God cursed the serpent by saying, "And I will put enmity between you and the woman, and between your offspring and hers; he will crush your head, and you will strike his heel."

Upon arriving in Moab Balak asks Balaam why he has not come sooner. Surely Balaam does not question Balak's resources, does he? (22:36-37) Balaam advises him that what matters is that he is there now, but also reminds him that he can only say what God allows him to say. The typology of the donkey and Balaam begins to be repeated with Balaam and Balak.

Balaam's First Oracle

After this exchange, Balak begins the preparations for Balaam to curse Israel. He sacrifices cattle and sheep, an integral part of the act of divination that shows up as a recurring theme in the narrative, and brings Balaam up to Bamoth Baal, an elevated place where he could see the edge of Israel's encampment (22:39-41).[12] Balaam requests seven more alters with seven bulls and seven rams to be sacrificed upon them, then tells Balak to wait while he goes off to meet with God (23:1-3).

God indeed meets with Balaam and puts a word in his mouth to proclaim to Balak (23:5). Unfortunately for Balak, the word from God is not what he desired. Balaam proclaims that he cannot curse those whom God has not cursed or denounce those whom the Lord has denounced (23:8). Instead, Balaam blesses Israel, recalling God's promise to increase Abraham's offspring in 23:10a: "Who can count the dust of Jacob or number even a fourth of Israel?"[13] God's promise holds true: in the face of certain cursing God has brought blessing. Balak is understandably perturbed, but Balaam reminds him that he can only say what God tells him to (23:11-12).

Balaam's Second Oracle

Balak evidences his stubborn streak by trying the same process of offerings again, thinking a change in location, the field of Zophim on the top of Pisgah, will lead to a change in outcome (23:13-14). Again, God puts a word in Balaam's mouth for him to relay to Balak (23:16). Here the theme of blessing recurs, accompanied by the assertion that God will not go back on his promises. He says in 23:19-20 "God is not human, that he should lie, not a human being, that he should change his mind. Does he speak and then not act? Does he promise and not fulfill? I have received a command to bless; he has blessed, and I cannot change it."

In addition, Balaam focuses on God's ruling presence with Israel, saying "The Lord their God is with them; the shout of the King is among them. The Lord brought them out of Egypt; they have the strength of a wild ox" (23:21-22). God's immutability and immanence provide ample basis for Balaam to proclaim Israel's invincibility in 23:23-24. Balak responds by telling Balaam not to say anything else, whether cursing or blessing, but Balaam again tells him that if the Lord gives him something to say, he must say it (23:25-26).

Balaam's Third Oracle

Balak obstinately tries a third time to create a setting where Balaam can curse Israel. He understands that he must change God's mind, not Balaam, and he reasons that taking Balaam to the top of Peor, from which he could see Israel in the wilderness, will effect that change (23:27-28; 24:2). As Balak ignores three clear signs from Balaam to stop what he is trying to do, the reader recalls how Balaam ignored three clear signs from his donkey to stop what he was trying to do. Balak's plans are frustrated by the Lord and Balaam is nothing more than a mute beast through whom the Lord is pleased to communicate.

Balak builds seven altars for Balaam once again, but this time Balaam has no need to try to divine how God will respond; he knows God will bless Israel (23:29-24:1). Instead, as he looks out at Israel encamped tribe by tribe, the Spirit of God comes upon him and speaks through him (24:2). Before God had given Balaam words to say, but now the Spirit himself speaks in him. This third oracle centers on the certainty that God will fulfill what he has promised to Israel. Now that he can see clearly, Balaam describes Israel's tents as beautiful, like gardens beside a river and aloes (or tabernacles) planted by the Lord (24:3-6).[14] Seeing Israel encamped around God's presence in the tabernacle

(Numbers 1-2; 24:2) causes Balaam to describe the nation as the temple of God, the dwelling place of God's glory.

Balaam adds to this Garden imagery in 24:7a: "Water will flow from their buckets; their seed will have abundant water." He describes Israel like a multitude of trees who multiply because of the abundance of water all around them. Balaam describes Israel like an expanding Garden of Eden, the growing center of God's glory. The imagery of plant seeds multiplying also reminds the reader of Abraham's physical seed multiplying.

Balaam also speaks of the outcome of God's rule over Israel in 24:7b: "His king will be higher than Agag, and his kingdom shall be exalted."[15] He goes in on 24:8 to say, "God brings him out of Egypt and is for him like the horns of the wild ox." Whereas before God had brought the nation of Israel out of Egypt, now Balaam replaces the nation with this king and says that God brought the king out of Egypt. In doing this Balaam uses the king as a representative of the nation. This king is also described as a lion in terminology reminiscent of the promised kingly line of Judah in Genesis 49:10 (Numbers 24:9a). Balaam finishes his blessing of Israel in the latter half of 24:9 by quoting Genesis 12:3: "Blessed are those who bless you, and cursed are those who curse you."

Balak grows angry at Balaam a third for blessing Israel again, striking his hands together in an image reminiscent of Balaam striking his donkey along the road (24:10; cf. 22:23, 25, 27). He tells Balaam to go home and that he will not be giving him any money (24:11). As Balak's responses mirrors his previous responses, so also Balaam's response matches what he has already told Balak: he cannot differ from the command of the Lord, no matter how much money he is offered (24:12-13). He promises to go back to his people, but before he departs he leaves Balak a parting message, his fourth oracle (24:14).

Balaam's Fourth Oracle

Balaam's last speech differs from his previous three in a few significant ways. First, no altars of divination are set up. This follows from the previous oracle when altars were constructed but left unused when the Spirit came upon Balaam (24:1-2). Second, Balaam introduces the oracle by saying, "let me warn you of what this people will do to your people in days to come." The Hebrew phrase translated as "in days to come" or "in the latter days" occurs only fourteen times in the Old Testament and indicates an eschatological perspective.[16] Thus, this last oracle concerns things that will happen in the future, in an eschatological setting.

Balaam introduces the oracle by presenting himself in a similar fashion to his introduction in the third oracle: he sees, hears, and knows clearly the things of God (24:15-16; cf. 24:3-4). With this acute sense, Balaam perceives a figure who will come in the future: "A star will come out of Jacob; a scepter will rise out of Israel. He will crush the foreheads of Moab, the skulls of all the people of Sheth" (24:17). Balaam references the scepter of Judah from Genesis 49:10[17] and describes the future ruler as a star as well. This verse also alludes to Genesis 3:15, where God promised that one of Eve's descendants would crush the head of Satan and his descendants. The king in Balaam's prophecy crushes the heads of Moab and Sheth, nations that are presented as seeds of the serpent because of their opposition to Israel.[18] The reference to Israel's victory over Moab flies in the face of Balak, Moab's king, but Balaam also prophecies dominion for Israel over Edom (who had denied them passage in 20:14-21), Amalek, the Kenites, Ashur, and Eber (24:18-24).[19] This future king, referenced again in 24:19, exercises dominion over all of God's enemies. With this final word of prophecy, Balaam returns to his house and Balak follows suit (24:25).

The careful reader of Numbers should walk away from this passage with a different perspective towards God's interaction with Israel than he or she previously possessed. While Numbers 1-20 presents Israel as a nation prime for judgment and destruction, the language God speaks through Balaam shows that he is not finished with his people. God will make good on his word. Against the backdrop of Israel's covenant failure, the narrative of Balaam showcases God's covenant faithfulness. It is as if Moses were a jewelry store clerk selling a diamond to an eager young man looking for an engagement ring. In order to showcase the brilliance and facets of the diamond, Moses places it against a dark black backdrop. The contrast of the black brings out the sparkling beauty of the diamond, just like the black hearts of Israel bring out the sparkling beauty of God's faithfulness.

Conclusion

The context of the Pentateuch traces God's dealings with humans from creation, the fall, promises of blessing to Abraham, the exodus, and the giving of the law from Mt. Sinai. As the story moves to Numbers, it becomes evident that Israel is incapable of obeying God to the extent they must, and frequent judgment occurs.

Coming to Numbers 22-24, the story seems to provide God an opportunity to deservedly curse Israel through the political and spiritual powers of the Middle East. However, he holds true to his promises to Israel by confounding Balak's efforts and usurping Balaam's words, turning this opportunity for cursing into an expansion of blessings to his chosen people.

Now that we have a good grasp on the preliminary information surrounding Numbers 22-24, we can dive into a thematic study of the story. This is the meat of biblical theology. The table is set; prepare for a feast.

Michael Dietzel

Part 2: Thematic Development

Michael Dietzel

Chapter 5

Blessing and Cursing

How do the authors of Numbers 22-24 (Moses and the second compiler directly, Balaam indirectly, God overarchingly) develop the storyline of the Scriptures? Throughout these chapters Balaam references numerous promises and prophecies found earlier in the Pentateuch. By adding more information to these previous themes, the authors both zero in and zoom out on the story. They zero in by adding details that help explain the specifics of what will happen in the future, removing the fuzziness from the picture of the Pentateuch clearing up the image of the story. They zoom out by expanding the promises already given and showing the readers that the picture of the

Pentateuch is bigger than previously expected.

Before we get into the themes, let me make a quick note concerning the structure of the next four chapters. The themes of blessing and cursing, a king from Judah, Israel as God's tabernacle, and the latter days are distinct, yet inseparable. They have discernably different traits, backgrounds, and developments, but they work together to communicate a meaning in this text.

It is like the movie *National Treasure,* in which Nicholas Cage's character uses a pair of Benjamin Franklin's bifocals to see a hidden treasure map on the back of the Declaration of Independence. The bifocals have several sets of lenses through which the document could be viewed: one green, one red, one blue, and several clear. When one lens is used, a certain part of the map showed up. However, when different combinations of lenses are put together, a more complete picture image is revealed.

The themes of Numbers 22-24 act as these bifocal lenses. When treated individually they help see important and necessary truths and portions of the big idea, but they must also be taken together. I will discuss each theme in a separate chapter, then provide a synthesis of the themes in chapter eight. The connectedness of the themes, however, forces each to be mentioned at some level in the discussion of the others.

Context

The theme of blessing and cursing provide overarching theme for Numbers 22-24.[1] Blessing and cursing language shows up a combined thirty-four times in these three chapters. At the beginning of the narrative, the context is set by Balak seeking to curse Israel and Balaam not being able to do so because God has blessed them (22:4-6, 12). Conversations that center on Balak desiring to curse Israel but Balaam only being able to say the words God gives him, which turn out to be blessings upon Israel, occur six times in the text and emphasize the main theme.[2]

This theme of blessing and cursing has its roots in previous texts in the Pentateuch. At the most basic level, blessing comes from having a right or special relationship with God. In Genesis 1:22 God blesses the creatures in the water and the creatures in the air by commanding them to be fruitful and fill the water and the air. In 1:28, God blesses mankind by commanding them to be fruitful, to fill the earth with offspring, and to exercise dominion over the animals and the land. God also blesses the seventh day of creation in 2:3, sanctifying it as a day of rest from his creative work. The themes of blessing and dominion are established early on.

As a result of Adam and Eve's rebellion and disobedience, the blessing and dominion are marred. Adam and Eve no longer have an appropriate relationship with God because of their sin. God exiles Adam and Eve from his presence in the Garden of Eden nd promises hardship for Adam, Eve, the serpent, and the earth (3:14-19). However, in the midst of these curses God promises that the seed of Eve would crush the head of the seed of the serpent. While Adam and Eve have failed to be fruitful and multiply and to exercise dominion so far, God promises that their descendants will succeed. And later in the story, this promise begins to come true as God commands one of Eve's descendants, Noah, to be fruitful and multiply (8:17; 9:1, 7), a task he and his descendants begin to fulfill. Chapter 10 provides a genealogy of Noah's immediate descendants, 11:1-9 describes how God spread those descendants over the earth, and 11:10-26 gives another genealogy of Noah's extended descendants over the course of several hundred years.

God pronounces five curses in Genesis 3-11 upon the serpent (3:14), the ground (3:17; 5:29), Cain (4:11), and Canaan (9:25).[3] The curses in these chapters are righteous judgments of God for the sinful actions of human beings. They reflect the state of God's relationship with humans, and the reflection is not good. However, these five curses are matched in Genesis 12:1-3, where God uses blessing language five times in three verses (2x in 12:2, 3x in 12:3).[4]

In Genesis 12:1-3, God approaches Abram and promises to bless him. God commands him to go to the land he will lead him and promises to grow him into a great nation, to bless him, and to bless all the people in the earth through him. The idea of blessing is certainly one of God's three promises to Abram, but it could also be considered as the overall thrust of all the promises as it shows up so frequently in the text. God has singled Abram out to have a special relationship with him, and blessing is the result.

God makes other promises to Abram that build upon his blessing in Genesis 12:1-3. In 13:14-17 God shows him the extent of the promised land, all Abram can see to the north, south, east, and west, and the extent of the number of his descendants, as many as the dust of the earth. This terminology reflects that God's blessing is hyperbolically large and will grow beyond physical land and descendants.

Genesis 14:18-20 tells of Melchizedek, king of Salem, proclaiming that Abram is blessed by God Most High and that God has delivered Abram's enemies into his hand. God reaffirms the promise to provide Abram with descendants in 15:4-5, this time describing them as being as many as the stars in the sky. The twin themes of fruitfulness and dominion occur again in the context of blessing. In 15:7-19 God makes an agreement to bring Abram into the land he promised by establishing a covenant with him. After Abram cuts a heifer, a goat, and a ram in half, significantly, only God, not Abram, passes between them, showing that God will keep this covenant regardless of Abram's, or his descendants', actions.

In 17:1-16 God commands Abram to walk before him in faithfulness and blamelessness, establishes the covenant of circumcision with him, and changes his name to Abraham. The commands and the covenant are significant because they

Michael Dietzel

highlight the human responsibility present in the relationship between Abraham and God. God will certainly bless him and his descendants, but Abraham and his descendants must also be obedient to God. In language reminiscent of the promise about Eve and her seed in 3:15, God promises in 17:6 to make Abraham and his seed fruitful and to establish their dominion over the earth by establishing nations and kings from them. In addition, the switch of name from Abram (exalted father) to Abraham (father of a multitude) highlights the fact that Abraham's descendants will be countless.

The Lord again mentions his promise to Abraham to make him a great nation and to bless all the nations of the earth through him in 18:18. He also promises to bless Abraham and his descendants, multiplying them to be as many as the number of the grains of sand on the seashore, to give them dominion over their enemies, and to bless all the nations of the earth through them in 22:17-18.

These promises begin go extend to Abraham's children when a wife is found for his son, Isaac. The family of Isaac's future wife, Rebekah, blesses Rebekah by wishing that her descendants would increase to be thousands upon thousands and that they would have dominion over their enemies. As people join the family of Abraham, the same promise of blessing extends to them as well.

After Abraham's death, the motif of blessing in the fruitfulness and dominion of his descendants continues. The blessing goes to Isaac and not Ishmael, following God's sovereign selection (21:11-13). The blessing goes to Jacob and not Esau again because of God's sovereign choice to have a unique relationship with Jacob (25:21-34; 27:1-28:9; Romans 9:10-13). When Isaac blesses his son Jacob in 27:27-29, he pronounces that Jacob will have dominion over the nations and echoes the promise of 12:3 by saying, "May those who curse you be cursed and those who bless you be blessed."

In 28:12-15 God appears to Jacob in a dream and promises him descendants and dominion: descendants like the dust of the earth who will spread out north, south, east, and west, and dominion over the land he had promised to Abraham and over all peoples. In 32:25-30 God changes Jacob's name to Israel. The nation formed by his descendants, who are also the descendants of Abraham, will come to be known by this name. God also blesses Israel in 35:9-13, commanding him to be fruitful and multiply and telling him that a nation, even a company of nations would come from him. He adds that kings will be among Israel's descendants, calling to mind the same promise to Abraham and Sarah in 17:6. When God made this promise to Israel, he had blessed Israel with twelve sons, but these sons would grow into an even greater multitude through the rest of the story.

One of Israel's sons, Joseph, becomes the focus of God's blessing in 39:1-6 as God gives Joseph dominion over the entire household of Potiphar, a high ranking Egyptian official. God not only gives Joseph this position but blesses him as he manages it.

Later, God through Potiphar makes Joseph second in command over all Egypt (41:41-43), nearly reaching kingly status (cf. 17:6; 35:11). These developments in the life of Joseph show the first fruits of fulfillment of God's promise to exercise dominion through the children of Abraham. At the end of Israel's life, he tells Joseph how God blessed Israel by promising him to increase his seed, develop nations from him, and give him the promised land as an everlasting possession (48:4). He then gives this blessing to Joseph's sons, Ephraim and Mannaseh, wishing that they would increase and multiply as well (48:9-21).

After blessing Joseph's sons, Israel blesses his own sons. He says "Gather around so I can tell you what will happen to you in days to come" (49:1). The temporal marker "days to come" (or "latter days") is also used in Numbers 24:14 and has important implications which will be discussed in detail in chapter 8. By proclaiming that these blessings would occur in the latter days, Israel signifies that they have an eschatological impact (having to do with the end times).

Two of these blessings stand out as most important. First, in 49:8-12 Israel says Judah will have dominion over his brothers, describing him as a lion. He also says that that the scepter will not depart from Judah, prophesying that from Judah's descendants will come kings (cf. 17:6; 35:11). Second, in 49:22-26 Israel describes Joseph in language overflowing with blessing and fruitfulness.[5] Interestingly, the name Judah has some connection with the idea of praise, while Joseph has some connection with increasing.[6]

Also interesting in this section of blessing are the curses Israel places upon several of his sons. To Reuben he says, "Turbulent as the waters, you will no longer excel, for you went up onto your father's bed, onto my couch and defiled it" (49:4). This is due to Rueben's sexual sin with his father's concubine in 35:22. To Simeon and Levi he adds, "Cursed be their anger, so fierce, and their fury, so cruel! I will scatter them in Jacob and disperse them in Israel" (49:7). This curse comes as a result of Simeon and Levi's murderous action in an attempt to uphold the honor of their sister Dinah in 34:1-31.

Israel adds that Issachar will be forced into labor (49:15), describes Dan as a snake that bites heels (49:17; cf. Genesis 3:15), and prophesies an attack on Gad (49:19). While the blessing, growth, and dominion God has promised to Abraham, Isaac, and Jacob will certainly continue through the descendants of Judah and Joseph, the theme of cursing because of disobedience also remains present.

After Genesis, the nation of Israel grows from seventy people to a multitude that covers the land (Exodus 1:1-7). When the nation cries out to God in their oppressed state, God remembers his covenant and leads them out of Egypt in the great Exodus (2:23-25; 5-14). In the narrative of the Exodus, we can see that the blessing to Abraham's descendants is realized in the nation of Israel. God chose Israel as his called-out people and entered into a special relationship with them (cf. Deuteronomy

3:47; 10:15). However, as has been already seen, as God gives the law to Israel so he can dwell with them in the tabernacle, they disobey and incur judgment upon themselves. In Numbers, this disobedience is highlighted, culminating in the nation's failure in Numbers 15-19 and 21 and Moses' failure in 20.

Development

Now that we have seen the origin of the blessing God promises to his people, let us discover how this theme is developed in the story of Balaam. From the first words of Numbers 22, the reader should recognize a clear allusion to Genesis 12:3 and the theme of blessing and cursing. When Balak seeks to buy Balaam's services to curse Israel, he describes the diviner's power by saying, "For I know that whoever you bless is blessed, and whoever you curse is cursed" (22:6). The attentive reader realizes that Balak is attributing to a human diviner a power that belongs only to God.

The sides are drawn: On one side, the God of Abraham, Isaac, and Jacob who has promised to bless those who bless Abraham's descendants. On the other side, Balaam, whom Balak believes has the ability to bless and to curse Israel. In the middle lies disobedient Israel, the potential object of the blessings and curses. The nation deserves to be cursed, and the question becomes whether God will continue to bless his disobedient people or if Balaam's power to curse will prevail.

The answer becomes clear almost as quickly as the

question is posed. God tells Balaam that he "must not put a curse on those people, because they are blessed" (22:12). God prevents a curse from befalling his people because they are a blessed people, and they are a blessed people because of their special relationship with him.[7] Even though Israel deserves to be cursed, and even though one with the supposed power to curse comes against them, God will not allow it. The beautiful facets of the diamond of God's faithfulness shine bright against the dark background of Israel's sinfulness and Balaam's power.

Moving forward in the narrative, Balaam begins his first oracle by describing the situation. Balak desires him to curse and denounce Israel, but how can he curse those whom God has not cursed? How can he denounce those whom the Lord has not denounced? (23:7-8).

He then looks at Israel and sees a nation distinct from other nations (23:9). He describes the nation in 23:10a by saying, "Who can count the dust of Jacob or number even a fourth of Israel?" Balaam paints Israel with hyperbolic language, saying he cannot even count a fourth of their population. This blessed nation has grown to the point that it can be described in the terminology God used in Genesis 13:26 and 28:4. As God told Abraham that his offspring would be like the dust of the earth, uncountable, Balaam sees them as the dust of the earth, even the fourth part uncountable. At the end of the first oracle, Balak notes that Balaam has blessed rather than cursed, and Balaam indicates that it is God who has done the blessing (23:11-12)

The beginning of the second oracle differs little from the first. Balaam again addresses Balak, reminding him that God is not a human who lies or changes his mind (23:19). God has commanded him to bless, not curse (23:20). In 23:21 he describes why Israel is blessed: "No misfortune is seen in Jacob, no misery observed in Israel. The LORD their God is with them; the shout of the King is among them." While God has promised to raise up kings from Abraham's descendants, (Genesis 17:6; 35:11; 49:8-12), now the Hebrew parallelism shows that God is acting as their king. However he also describes them as a lion in 23:24, recalling the imagery of the dominion of Judah the lion in Genesis 49:9-10. In 23:22-23, Balaam proclaims that Israel is blessed because of God's hand in their history, remembering the Exodus and pointing to God's work among them. Balak tells Balaam not to curse or bless, but Balaam reminds him of his divine mandate to bless (23:25-26).

Balaam's third oracle differs from the first two because rather than seeking omens and divination to determine what God would have him say, he understood that God would bless Israel (24:1). In addition, the Spirit comes upon him to deliver his message (24:2). Here he describes Israel's encampments in terminology reminiscent of the Garden of Eden, language that will be developed in chapter 7 of this work. He also draws on multiplication imagery as he says in 24:7a, "Water will flow from their buckets; their seed will have abundant water."

In 24:7b-9 he uses kingly dominion language. First, in

24:7b he says that Israel's king will be higher than Agag and that Israel's kingdom will be exalted. Second, in 24:8a he makes a similar statement to 23:22: "God brings him out of Egypt and is for him like the horns of the wild ox" (ESV).[8] While in 23:22 Balaam seems to speak about God bringing Israel out of Egypt, in 24:8a he seems to speak about God bringing one person, a king, out of Egypt. In 24:8b-9a he uses dominion and lion language to describe this person, recalling Genesis 49:8-12. He then closes his oracle in 24:9b by quoting Genesis 12:3 almost word for word: "May those who bless you be blessed and those who curse you be cursed." Balak is again incensed, telling Balaam to return to his home, but Balaam reminds him that he is only speaking the words God has given him.

Post-Numbers Expansion

The themes of blessing and cursing spread out far and wide after Numbers 22-24. Deuteronomy, which comes directly after Numbers, uses blessing and cursing language extensively.[9] In chapter 7, Moses echoes the promise given to Abraham by telling Israel that if they are obedient, God will bless and multiply them (7:12-16). 28:1-14 describes the blessings Israel would receive for their obedience, but these verses are sandwiched between chapter 27 and 28:15-68 that describe the curses Israel would receive for their disobedience. Specifically, 28:36-68 describes in graphic language the extent Israel would be cursed if they fell away from God: exile. Sadly, the nation of God's blessing did rebel against him and God righteously cursed them by sending them into exile.

But despite Israel's disobedience, God was not done with his blessing. Isaiah 19 contains the prophet's charge against Egypt. The nation that opposes (curses) Israel will be cursed for its opposition (19:1-15). But verse 16 marks a turn in the prophet's tone towards Egypt. In a future day (19:16, 18, 19, 21, 23, 24) God will bring Egypt into a relationship with himself. Concluding this prophecy, Isaiah links Israel with Assyria and Egypt and describes them as "a blessing on the earth" (19:24). In verse 25 he says, "The Lord Almighty will bless them, saying, 'Blessed be Egypt my people, Assyria my handiwork, and Israel my inheritance.' " This shows an expansion of blessing from Israel, now in exile, to other nations on the earth. Later, in chapter 61, Isaiah writes about the future year of the Lord's favor (61:2). In this passage he mentions that the offspring and descendants who enjoy this year of the Lord's favor are blessed by the Lord (61:9).

Blessing and cursing language continues into the New Testament. In Luke 4:16-21, Jesus reads from Isaiah 61:1-2 and proclaims that it was fulfilled, implicitly saying that he was the anointed one who would bring the blessings of the year of the Lord's favor.[10] Jesus' life, death, and resurrection provide the greatest blessing for his people: eternal life through belief in him (John 20:29-31).

In Acts 3, Peter explains this concept to a group of Jews in

Solomon's Colonnade, showing them that Jesus, whom the Jews had killed, was truly the Messiah. At the culmination of his argument he references God's promise to Abraham, stating that God sent his servant Jesus to bless the Jews first by providing them this blessing, which was salvation (3:25-26).

In Galatians 3, Paul argues against turning to the law to be justified by explaining that those who believe in Christ are blessed with the blessing of Abraham, which is justification through Jesus' death (3:8-9). He adds that those who rely on the law are under a curse, but blessing comes through faith in Christ Jesus who became a curse himself by being hung on a tree (3:10-13). In becoming a curse, Christ redeems those who believe in him, ensuring that the blessing of Abraham, salvation, would go to the Gentiles.

In Ephesians 1:3-14, Paul explains that God himself is blessed for having blessed believers in the heavenly realms with every spiritual blessing in Christ (1:3). He receives blessing in the form of praise because he has blessed his people. Paul goes on to explain what blessings God's people receive by describing six aspects of salvation: election (1:4), predestination (1:5), redemption, which is the forgiveness of sins (1:7), unity of all things (1:10), inheritance (1:11), and the seal of the Holy Spirit (1:13-14). All of these blessings are in Christ (1:3, 4, 6, 7, 9, 10, 11, 12, 13), showing that the blessing of Abraham finds realization in the salvation Jesus provides.

Conclusion

God's blessing to Adam, to Abraham, and to Israel features prominently in the Balaam narratives, as does the cursing of the disobedient and those who curse God's blessed ones. This blessing and cursing is reaffirmed, showing that God will not forsake his promises to bless and curse. The Balaam narrative zeroes in on this theme by showing that even when given an opportunity to curse, God will still bless his people. By reflecting on the massive size of the nation, Balaam shows that God remains faithful to keep his promises to Abraham and his descendants. The narrative also zooms out on this theme by connecting the theme of blessing to the lion and scepter that would come from Judah, a single person viewed in connection with the entire nation, a person who would be Jesus Christ. Now Gentiles and Jews are a part of God's blessing, salvation by grace through faith in Jesus Christ.

Chapter 6

The King from Judah

Though not as prevalent as the idea of blessing and cursing, there are several direct and indirect references to a king from the tribe of Judah in Numbers 22-24. Just like the Balak's attempts to get Balaam, a spiritual power, to curse Israel are contrasted with the power and promise of God to bless his chosen people, King Balak stands opposed to the appropriate reign that God has over the nation of Israel. In the face of the highest political power, God displays his sovereign rule and provides information concerning what his reign will look like in the future.

As with the theme of blessing and cursing, the theme of a

king from Judah finds its origins earlier in the Pentateuch and sees its outcome expanded in later material in the prophets and apostles. The references to a king in these chapters tie together several previously unconnected motifs and give a better picture of the theme of kingship and dominion in the Scriptures. The seemingly unconnected themes will be mentioned first and then the treatment of Numbers 22-24 will explain why they should be seen together. Finally, the unified theme will be traced through the rest of the Old Testament and the New Testament to see how authors after the Pentateuch used it.

Context

The first relevant motif occurs in Genesis 3:15. When God curses Satan, he says, "I will put enmity between you and the woman, and between your offspring and hers; he will crush your head, and you will strike his heel." The key element in relation to Numbers 22-24 is the idea of the seed of the woman crushing the head of the seed of the serpent. The motif of crushing the head is an ultimate sign of dominance, dominion, and victory, and in Genesis 3 God promises that the seed of the woman will have this dominance, dominion, and victory over Satan and his seed (those who follow in the path of Satan).

The origins of a second motif appear in the narrative of Abram. In Genesis 15:5 God tells Abram to look up at the stars and try to count them. He then promises that his offspring will be as numerous as the stars, using a metaphor to show that Abram's descendants will be exceedingly great in number. God makes this promise again to Abraham in Genesis 22:17 and to Isaac in 26:4. The relationship between Abraham's descendants and celestial beings shows up once more in Genesis 37:9 where Joseph dreams that his father, mother, and brothers, represented by the sun, moon, as stars, bow down to him.

A third motif also finds its origins in the Abrahamic narrative. God mentions kings for the first time in relation to blessing Israel in Genesis 17:6 when he promises that kings will be among the descendants of Abraham. While prior to this God had promised numerous descendants and blessings (Genesis 12:1-3; 13:16, 15:1-5), now he specifies that from the uncountable sand of Abraham's descendants some would become kings over nations. This was part of the blessing given to Abraham and an expansion of God's intended promise. The same promise is given again in Genesis 35:11, this time to Jacob instead of Abraham.

The story of Joseph coming to power echoes this promise, though Joseph was not exalted fully as the true king of Egypt (Genesis 41:41-43). However, it is in the context of the Joseph narratives that the primary text regarding the reign of a member of the tribe of Judah occurs. In the blessings given by Jacob to his sons in Genesis 49, Jacob refers to Judah in kingly terminology. He ascribes to him dominion over his brothers and his enemies in verse 8, but the most memorable imagery occurs in verses 9 and 10. He first says in 9, "You are a lion's cub, Judah, you return from the prey, my son. Like a lion he crouches and lies down, like a lioness – who dares to rouse him?" Using the royal imagery of the lion, the king of the animal world, Jacob describes Judah as a lion. He adds in verse 10, "The scepter will not depart from Judah, nor the ruler's staff from between his feet, until he to whom it belongs shall come and the obedience of the nations shall be his." Jacob attributes reigning power to Judah, a power that will not depart until the one to whom it truly belongs comes.

The three images of dominion, a lion, and the scepter unite to create the picture of a line of reigning kings who would descend from Judah.

The scope of the fourth and last motif is much wider than the previous three. One of the greatest overarching themes of the Bible as a whole is the presence of God with his people. Starting in the Garden of Eden, God communes with his image-bearers in right relationship. The disobedience of Adam and Eve results in God having to cast them out of his presence, placing a barrier between humans and their creator.

However, God loves his people and desires to dwell with him, and this desire acts as an underlying motive for his actions in the narrative of the Pentateuch. God enters into a covenant with Abraham, gives him descendants, takes the family of Jacob to Egypt, enslaves the nation of Israel, and brings them out of slavery and to the foot of Mt. Sinai as part of his plan to dwell once again with his people. He tells Moses in Exodus 25:8, "Then have them make a sanctuary for me, and I will dwell among them." Chapters 25-32 and 35-40 are filled with instructions regarding the precise construction of the tabernacle and the establishment of a priesthood to keep it.

In the midst of these instructions God reveals his intentions behind the construction of a tabernacle: "Then I will dwell among the Israelites and be their God. They will know that I am the LORD their God, who brought them out of Egypt so that I might dwell among them. I am the LORD their God' (Exodus 29:45-46). The promise of God's presence becomes a reality in Exodus 40:34-38, when the glory of God descends upon Israel and fills the tabernacle. His presence then directs the Israelites as they move towards the promised land. God once again dwells with his people.

However, this dwelling was incomplete. Only the priesthood could come into God's presence, and only infrequently and after copious amounts of purification. God's plan was incomplete; something more was in store. This can be seen by what God tells Moses in Leviticus 26:11-13. He says that if Israel is obedient and follows his commands, "I will put my dwelling place among you, and I will not abhor you. I will walk among you and be your God, and you will be my people." This looks forward to a day when God will dwell with his people in a better way.

Development

These four motifs all appear in Numbers 22-24. In Balaam's second oracle, he says "The LORD their God is with them; the shout of the King is among them" (Numbers 23:21). The first reference to a king in this narrative names God as a king, specifically a king who is among the people. This links the idea that God desires to dwell with his people with the idea of the promised king. Here the king is not a human, but rather God himself, an idea that does not seem to make sense with the previous promise of a king. This idea will continue to be developed and explained both here and future stories.

The presence of God as king with his people comes with blessings for Israel, as they encounter no misfortune or misery (23:21) and divination and omens are powerless against them (23:23; especially poignant given Balak's desires for Balaam to curse Israel). God's presence with Israel is accented by the reference to his leadership in bringing them out of Egypt, giving them the strength of a wild ox (23:22).

The animal metaphor is switched in 23:24 as Balaam compares Israel to a lion who devours its prey and drinks the blood of its enemies. Balaam applies the kingly picture of a lion to the entire nation of Israel rather than one person. Both the king and the nation can be represented with a lion, a symbol both of the ruling power of the ruler and the nation he rules. This seems to indicate a relationship between one person, here a specific descendant of Judah who will reign as king over the nation, and the nation of Israel as a whole. The relationship between God as king and both the nation of Israel and one specific descendant of Judah referred to as a lion-king is left unexplained in these chapters but finds important development later in Scripture.

The next mention of a king comes in Balaam's third oracle. As he describes Israel as a lush garden filled with beautiful trees and flowing water, he adds that, "his king shall be higher than Agag, and his kingdom shall be exalted" (24:7). This is followed immediately by a statement nearly identical to the one found in 23:22: "God brings him out of Egypt and is for him like the horns of the wild ox; he shall eat up the nations, his adversaries, and shall break their bones in pieces and pierce them through with his arrows" (24:8). Again Balaam makes reference to the exodus, focusing on the dominion God gives to his people over their enemies.

However, this time the objective pronoun in question is singular, not plural. While God brings *them* out of Egypt in 23:22 he brings *him* out of Egypt in 24:8. In both cases Israel is the object, but in 23:22 the nation is referred to as a group of people while in 24:8 Israel is referred to as one person. As in 23:23, when Israel bore the title of lion, the plurality and singularity of Israel are used interchangeably. This idea of corporate solidarity is often used in Hebrew literature and shows the connection between a single person and the group he or she represents.[1]

This shift from plural to singular in Numbers 23-24 shows the marks of intentional authorship. As Balaam prophesies and Moses and the second author compile this material, they show that the future king from Judah will represent the whole nation by participating in a greater, future exodus.

Lion imagery shows up in Balaam's third oracle as well, where is says in 24:9, "He crouched, he lay down like a lion and like a lioness; who will rouse him up?" This is followed in verse 10 by a quotation of Genesis 12:3; "Blessed are those who bless you, and cursed are those who curse you." In this section Balaam unites the promise of a lion-king from Judah with the blessing of Abraham, showing that the two are significantly linked. The blessing of Abraham will come in large part through the reign of his descendants.

The last mention of the king occurs in Balaam's final oracle. Balaam gives insightful information in this vision by stating that what he sees will occur in the latter days (24:14). He says that he now has his eyes opened and can see the vision of the Lord clearly (24:15-16). Then he tells Balak what it is that he sees in verse 17: "I see him, but not now; I behold him, but not here. A star will come out of Jacob; a scepter will rise out of Israel. He will crush the foreheads of Moab, the skulls of all the people of Sheth." The star from Jacob is reminiscent of God's promise to Abraham and Isaac to make their descendants like the stars of the sky in Genesis 15:5, 22:17, and 26:4 and Joseph's dream of his brothers as stars in 37:9.

In these stories the descendants of Abraham as a whole in God's promise and the fathers of the twelve tribes in Joseph's dream were pictured as stars, while in Balaam's proclamation one singular star will come out of Jacob. These stories also bring up the idea of corporate solidarity, as a metaphor for the entire nation is applied to a singular person.

The star coming out of Jacob is paralleled with a scepter rising out of Jacob. This scepter is a clear allusion to Genesis 49:10. The scepter that would not depart from Judah appears again in Balaam's vision. Both the star and the scepter point to a person, someone who will crush the head of Moab and the skulls of Sheth. The reference to this person crushing the heads of his enemies points back to Genesis 3:15 and boldly states that this star, this scepter of Judah, will be the one to finally crush Satan. The fact that this will occur in the latter days solidifies this claim.

It is clear that this dominion applies to more than just Moab and Sheth. Rather it refers to God's enemies in general, because in 24:18-25 Balaam gives an extensive, though not comprehensive list of the enemies the star of Jacob will conquer. Rather than taking this to mean that he will only have dominion over these enemies, it is better to view them as placeholders referring to all of the enemies of Israel. It is intentional, however, that the first of these enemies listed is Moab, the enemy currently trying to defeat Israel. King Balak will not be successful now or at any time.

Post-Numbers Expansion

The themes mentioned above occur both together and separately after Numbers 22-24. The theme of the seed of the woman crushing the head of the seed of the serpent appears throughout the history of Israel. It can be seen in God providing children to women like Ruth in Ruth 4 or Hannah in 1 Samuel 1, children who would go on to serve the Lord and defeat the seed of the serpent by their obedience. It can also be seen quite literally in the stories of Jael and Sisera in Judges 4 and David and Goliath in 1 Samuel 17 where two seeds of the woman drive a stake through and cut off the heads of two seeds of the serpent respectively.

Both Psalm 2 and Psalm 110 speak of the dominion given to God's chosen one over his enemies. Psalm 2 paints the picture of the nations and kings of the earth conspiring against God and his anointed one (Psalm 2:1-3). But God has established his king on Mt. Zion (2:6) and the power of the kings of the earth pales in comparison to his power. Interestingly this king is referred to as God's son in 2:7. This king, God's son, the anointed one, inherits the nations and crushes the head of his enemies (2:8-9).

Psalm 110 opens with God giving dominion and authority to the lord of the speaker (110:1). God extends this person's scepter in the act of ruling (110:2) and crushes kings and nations for him (110:5-6), referencing Genesis 49:10 and 3:15 respectively. These chapters are important links to these themes and are themselves referenced in other passages throughout Scripture.

One of the most important figures in regards to this theme is David. As God's anointed one (1 Samuel 16:13; cf. Psalm 2:2), David comes to power as the king of Israel and asserts his dominance and dominion over his enemies as he expands the boundaries of his nation. David fulfills at least partially the kingly figure spoken about in Numbers 22-24 as a king from Judah who crushes the heads of his enemies. Though the prophecy about the king defeating Agag finds more relevance in the story of Samuel killing Agag, king of the Amalekites, in 1 Samuel 15:33, David defeats the Amalekites himself in 1 Samuel 30. Where Saul failed to kill Agag, resulting in Samuel having to fulfill his duty for him, David crushed the heads of his enemies.[2] Ironically, David descends from a Moabite woman, Ruth. The one whom Balaam prophesies would crush the foreheads of Moab (Numbers 24:17) turns out to be a descendant of Moab.

However David is not the final fulfillment of these prophecies. This is evidenced by the promise God gives David in 2 Samuel 7. God promises to establish David's house, to keep his descendants on the throne as kings and rulers. Because of God's promise, David's house, kingdom, and throne will last forever (2 Samuel 7:16). Though David himself will not live and reign forever, like Abraham his descendants after him will carry on his legacy. David is a king from Judah who crushes the heads of his enemies, and his reign narrows the focus regarding the king from Judah to someone specifically from the line of David, someone like David himself. 2 Samuel 7 shows that the prophecies of Numbers 22-24 are not yet finally fulfilled.

Micah 5 contains another important prophecy in relation to David. Chapter 5 verse 2 speaks of a ruler who will come out of Bethlehem, the city of David's birth, also identified as one of the lesser towns of the clans of Judah. This ruler is special, however, because his origins are from old, from ancient times. The ruler, a son of Israel, will be a shepherd and will rule in the strength of the LORD and the majesty of his name (5:4). He will bring peace to the nation by crushing the heads of his enemies (5:5-6). In another link to Numbers 22-24, Israel, under this ruler, is identified as a lion who conquers the animals around him (5:8).

Isaiah 7 and 9 link David's reign to the presence of God with his people. Isaiah 7:14 foretells of a child who will be born of a virgin who will be called Immanuel, meaning God with us. Immanuel is mentioned in Isaiah 8:8 and 10, and God is mentioned as Israel's king in 8:21. Isaiah 9:6-7 once again picks up the idea of a child being born, and shows that "He will reign on David's throne and over his kingdom, establishing and upholding it with justice and righteousness from that time on and forever." The eternal throne of David promised in 2 Samuel 7 will come to be through a baby called Immanuel, God with us.

Jeremiah 30 focuses on the nature of the restoration of Israel after the exile to Babylon (30:3). The discussion is also framed by day of the Lord language (30:3, 7, 8) and, importantly, latter days language (30:24). This mention of the latter days ties directly to Numbers 24:14 and shows that the two prophecies are linked. In the day of their restoration, God says that Israel will "serve the LORD their God and David their king whom I will raise up for them." Because David has died and been buried, this does not refer to the literal person of David, but rather one like him, a type, a descendant of David who will be on the throne forever (cf.

2 Samuel 7). This future David will take up the scepter of Judah (Numbers 24:17) and lead Israel in their restoration to blessing from the Lord. 30:21 affirms that this Davidic king will come from their midst and be an Israelite himself.

Jeremiah 30 also ties the idea of God being with his people to the idea of a Davidic, Judaic king ruling over Israel. In 30:11 the Lord declares, "I am with you and will save you," and in 30:22 he says "So you will be my people, and I will be your God."[3] Micah 5 and Jeremiah 30 speak in the same way as Numbers 22-24, affirming both God's kingly presence among his people and the reality of the king's identification with his people. These chapters take the theme of the scepter from Judah coming to crush his enemies and apply it specifically to the reign of the future David who will bring restoration to his people.

Another important place in which these themes occur is Ezekiel 37. Following the account of God breathing a Spirit of new life into a valley of dry bones (37:1-14), God speaks a word of restoration for Israel and Judah (37:15-28). In 37:22 he promises to unite them under one king and make them a unified kingdom. He adds in 37:23 "They will be my people and I will be their God," echoing the same sentiments as Jeremiah 30:22. Then God identifies David as the king and shepherd who will reign over his people forever (37:24-25; cf. 2 Samuel 7). God will make a covenant with his people forever under King David, and the restored relationship leads to God making his dwelling place with his people, he being their God, and they being his people (37:26-

27). His presence with the people will make Israel holy forever (37:28). Much like Jeremiah 30 and Numbers 22-24, Ezekiel 37 ties together the themes of a Davidic king who reigns and God who is present with his people.

Throughout the Old Testament God is referred to as a king, much as he is in Numbers 23:21. He has the title Jacob's King in Isaiah 41:21 and he is called Israel's Holy One, Israel's Creator, and their King, respectively, in 43:15. Zephaniah 3:15 labels God as the King of Israel and adds that he is with his people, combining God's presence with his people with the reign of a king much like Numbers 22-24, Jeremiah 30, and Ezekiel 37. Malachi 1:14 also identifies God as a great king.

The last important Old Testament passages for this theme come from the book of Hosea. First, in chapter 3, Hosea uses the illustration of his wife Gomer representing unfaithful Israel to speak about the nation's future. After Gomer acts as an adulteress, removing herself from the leadership of her husband, the Lord commands Hosea to ransom her and bring her back. Hosea records this interaction in 3:1-3, then applies it to Israel in 3:4-5. He says, "For the Israelites will live many days without king or prince, without sacrifice or sacred stones, without ephod or household gods. Afterward, the Israelites will return and seek the LORD their God and David their king. They will come trembling to the LORD and to his blessings in the last days."

These verses point to a future Davidic king who will come when Israel returns to the Lord in the latter days, picking up on the kingly and eschatological themes from Balaam's oracles and showing that they will take place at a time of repentance and restoration.

The other important passage in Hosea occurs in chapter 11. The Lord, speaking through Hosea, uses the image of a child to refer to Israel. In 11:1 he says, "When Israel was a child, I loved him, and out of Egypt I called my son." This mention of the Exodus with Israel as a singular *he* calls to mind the similar mention of the Exodus with Israel as a singular he by Balaam in Numbers 24:8. Another link between the two chapters is found in Hosea 11:9, where God says, "I am God, and not a man – the Holy One among you." This calls to mind Numbers 23:19, which says "God is not human, that he should lie, not a human being that he should change his mind." As in Numbers where God refuses to change his mind and curse the people, so in Hosea God will not abandon his people for their sin but will restore them. Hosea 11:9 also echoes Numbers 23:21, which emphasizes the presence of God with his people. Hosea 11:10 goes on to refer to God as a lion, further linking the two passages together.

Hosea 3 and 11 are not the only places in which the prophet echoes Numbers 22-24, showing that he had Balaam's oracles in mind as he wrote his own work. Hosea 1:10 describes Israel as being as many as the sand of the sea and 4:7 focuses on Israel increasing (the same idea as Numbers 23:10). 2:15-16 says Israel will have vineyards in a future day and 10:1 describes Israel as a fruitful vine (Numbers 24:5-7, 14). 5:14 and 13:7 (along with

11:10, already mentioned) refer to God as a lion in Israel's midst (Numbers 23:22, 24; 24:9). Kings and princes are mentioned in 1:11; 7:3, 5, 7, 16; 8:4, 10; 10:3, 7, 15; 11:5; and 13:10-11 (Numbers 23:21; 24:7, 17; kings are also pictured in 3:4-5, mentioned above). 9:10 refers to the incident at Baal-Peor which occurred in Numbers 25 and has been attributed to the hand of Balaam.

The abundance and importance of these passages in Hosea shows conclusively that he intentionally draws on the themes of Numbers 22-24 and places their fulfillment in a time of restoration for Israel.

All of these references, specifically Hosea 11, provide a perfect jumping point to the New Testament development of this theme, for they link Numbers 22-24 with Matthew 2. The second chapter of Matthew picks up after the birth of Jesus, a descendant of Abraham, Judah, and David (Matthew 1:1-3, 6), in Bethlehem, the town of David. Already the context of Matthew 2 has links to Genesis 12:1-3, 49:10, Numbers 24:17, and Micah 5:2 and 8. In addition, Matthew 1:22-23 references Isaiah 7:14, which promised that a son would be born who would be called Immanuel, God with us. The presence of God with his people also plays into the context of Matthew 2.

Thus, it should come as no surprise that Matthew 2 also contains many references to and developments from Numbers 22-24. Two characters are introduced in Matthew 2:1: A pagan king and a group of pagan magicians.[4] These magicians come from the east and meet with the king. They are following a star that marks out the king of the Jews.

These details are nearly identical to the story of the pagan king Balak and the pagan magician from the east Balaam and show Matthew's intentional hand in shaping the story in such a way as to draw the reader's attention to Balaam's oracles. It is even probable that the Magi themselves had knowledge of the Numbers 24:17 prophecy about the star of Jacob coming to reign and rule which informed their journey to see this king of the Jews.[5]

The Magi find out from Micah 5:2 and 4 that the star marking the king of the Jews is leading them to Bethlehem, the town of David (Matthew 2:3-6). The pagan King Herod tries to destroy God's chosen people by means of these magicians, but God directly intervenes in the travels of the magicians and preserves Jesus and his family (Matthew 2:7-8, 12; cf. Numbers 22). The intentional hand of Matthew in recording these events shows that he interpreted the star of Jacob as referring to Jesus.

As the seed of Abraham, the scepter from Judah, the star of Jacob, and the descendant of David, Jesus fulfills the prophecy of Numbers 22-24. He is God with his people who will reign as king and crush the head of his enemies.

The latter half of Matthew 2 also affirms this. After the Magi leave, Herod seeks to kill all infants under the age of two (Matthew 2:16). Because of this, the Lord directs Joseph to take his family to Egypt during the time of persecution. Matthew then applies Hosea 11:1 to these circumstances, saying that the phrase, "out of Egypt I called my son" is fulfilled in them. This has frustrated many students of Scripture because the quotation in Hosea points to Israel as a nation being called out of Egypt and does not seem to be a prophecy pointing forward to an actual son being brought out of Egypt. This interpretation is often understood as Matthew either exercising his rights as an inspired apostle or typologically connecting the two passages.[6] Others argue that while Hosea intended one meaning, the Holy Spirit had a fuller meaning that did apply directly to Christ that he revealed to Matthew, though Hosea was unaware.[7]

However, these interpretive problems can be alleviated when Matthew's understanding of Hosea and Numbers, and in turn Hosea's understanding of Numbers, is considered. As has been already seen, Hosea intentionally draws links to Balaam's oracles. Specifically, Hosea 11:1 pulls from Numbers 24:8. Numbers 24:8, in turn, intentionally contrasts with Numbers 23:22. In 23:22 God brings *them*, the nation of Israel, out of Egypt, while in 23:8 God brings *him*, the nation of Israel, out of Egypt. Hosea 11:1 also refers to the Exodus as God bringing his singular son out of Egypt.

Given the previously seen connections between Matthew 2 and Numbers 22-24, it should be accepted that, in accordance with the corporate solidarity present in the Old Testament, Matthew agrees with Hosea in interpreting the pronominal change to refer to a singular figure serving as a representative of the nation who would lead them into a greater Exodus.[8]

This is supported by the fact that Jesus is represented as a better Israel in the opening chapters of Matthew. He is shown to be a descendant of Abraham (1:1-2) and an infant who escaped the tyrannical attempt to destroy Israelite infants (2:16-18; cf. Exodus 1:15-2:10). He spends the beginning of his life in Egypt but returns to dwell in the promised land (2:19-23; cf. Genesis 15:13-15). The presence of God in the form of the Spirit dwells with him and he undergoes testing in the wilderness for forty days, paralleling the forty years of testing of Israel (3:16-4:11; cf. Exodus 40:34-38; Numbers 14:26-35). He then chooses twelve disciples to parallel the twelve tribes of Israel, and delivers a sermon on the conduct of God's people on a mountain, just as God had delivered the law to Israel on Mt. Sinai (4:18-22; 5:1-7:29; cf. Exodus 19-31).

Jesus is presented as the better Israel, the star of Jacob, and the one whom God brings out of Egypt to lead his people and crush the heads of his enemies.

This also gives further explanation to the references of God as king in Numbers 23:21 and elsewhere, for in Jesus, God comes down and becomes a human, taking on the role of the new King David, the scepter of Judah. Jesus, the human king of Israel, is also the God-king. John writes similarly, describing in the first verse of his gospel that Jesus was God incarnated as man. He also ties together this theme with the theme of God dwelling with his people in John 1:14, describing that God became flesh and dwelt among his people. This verse will be considered more fully below, but for now it is sufficient to say that in Jesus' kingly reign, God is among his people. Numbers 23:21 finds fulfillment in Jesus Christ.

The final New Testament passage to be considered is found in Revelation. After Jesus comes and physically dwells with his people, the ultimate fulfillment of Jesus dwelling among humans (Revelation 21:1-4), he identifies himself to the churches. In 22:16 he says, "I, Jesus, have sent my angel to give you this testimony for the churches. I am the Root and the Offspring of David, and the bright Morning Star." Not only does Jesus identify himself as a king descended from David, he claims to be a star. This is a clear reference to Numbers 22-24 and specifically 24:17, referencing both the scepter of Israel and the star of Jacob.

This also recalls a previous identification of Jesus in Revelation 5:5: "Then one of the elders said to me, 'Do not weep! See, the Lion of the tribe of Judah, the Root of David, has triumphed. He is able to open the scroll and its seven seals.' " According to Revelation, Jesus is the Lion and scepter of Judah, the Root of David, and the Star of Jacob. Jesus fulfills these prophecies both in his life on earth two thousand years ago and in the future when he returns to earth.

Conclusion

The themes of a coming king, a lion and scepter of Judah, and God's presence with his people are themes from the beginning of the Pentateuch that are drawn together in Numbers 22-24. Balaam's oracles zero in on these themes by signaling their certainty as they are pronounced in the presence of a pagan king. God will provide a king who will crush the heads of all God's enemies. These chapters also zoom out on these themes by connecting them with each other and adding in a new theme: a star. Balaam presents the idea of a king who would come from Judah, a ruling lion, a royal scepter, and a glorious star, and ties them all together with the motif of God dwelling with Israel.

These themes find their fulfillment in Jesus Christ. The Old Testament passages that develop the ideas of Numbers 22-24 point forward to Jesus' ministry. The covenant of peace in Ezekiel 37 is inaugurated by Jesus' death. The restoration promised in Jeremiah 30 and Hosea 11 is accomplished in Christ. The union of Christ and his people in intimate dwelling comes from Jesus making his dwelling among men (John 1:1, 14; 2 Corinthians 6:16-18). The reign of God over his people can be seen in Numbers 22-24 as he leads them to victory over Balak, king of Moab, but it can be seen in greater fashion as Jesus claims victory over Satan at the cross.

Michael Dietzel

Chapter 7

Israel as God's Tabernacle

A third major theme present in the Pentateuch and developed in Numbers 22-24 is that of God's dwelling place. The discussion of this theme overlaps the previous discussion of God's kingship as it relates to God's dwelling with Israel as their king, but the subject matter will diverge from the discussion above in key aspects. The main passage referring to God's dwelling place with his people focuses on garden and temple imagery. This will be the center of the following discussion.

Context

When God creates the heavens and the earth and

everything within them, he creates a place where he could dwell with his first children, Adam and Eve. This is the original dwelling place of God with humans and is intended to be the context for Adam and Eve to extend God's dominion and glory to the ends of the earth.[1] When God tells Adam and Eve in Genesis 1:28 to "be fruitful and increase in number; fill the earth and subdue it," it can be implied that God's desire is to see his image-bearers extend the boundaries of their rule and the garden beyond their current limits. God wants the physical boundaries of the Garden of Eden to expand in order for his glory to be expanded as well

In addition to Adam and Eve serving as under-rulers for God in the garden, they also serve as the prototypical priests in God's first temple.[2] The verbs "cultivate" and "keep" used in Genesis 2:15 as Adam and Eve's job description in the garden are also used in reference to priests working in the tabernacle and temple.[3] As Adam and Eve rule and keep the garden, they are to worship God by extending the temple and bringing more and more of the earth under his dominion.

However, Adam and Eve prove to be unfaithful rulers and priests as they disobey God in Genesis 3 and are cast from the garden. God no longer dwells with his people in his first temple, but places a divide between himself and their sin, signified by the presence of an angel with a fiery sword at the eastern entrance of the garden (Genesis 3:23-24). However, given the promise of Genesis 3:15 (mentioned above in chapter 4) regarding the seed of the woman who would crush the head of the seed of the serpent, Adam and Eve have hope that God would restore his dwelling with them and their descendants.

God begins this process in earnest when he promises to bring Abraham into a new land (Genesis 12:1-3). Though the nation which will descend from Abraham will first spend four hundred years in Egypt (Genesis 15:13-16), God brings them out in the great event of the Exodus. In the events preceding the Exodus, God reveals to Moses, "I will be with you" (Exodus 3:12), pointing to the former dwelling God had with Adam and Eve and the eventual restoration of that dwelling. This is further evidenced in God's words to Pharaoh regarding the purpose of the plagues in Exodus 9:16: "But I have raised you up for this very purpose, that I might show you my power and that my name might be proclaimed in all the earth." As in the Garden of Eden, God's goal in the Exodus is to extend his glory and name to the ends of the earth.

God's glory becomes visibly present with his people in two ways during the Exodus narrative. First, Exodus 13:21-22 shows that God led Israel out of Egypt in a pillar of cloud during the day and a pillar of fire during the night. Second, and more importantly, Exodus 25-32 and 35-40 give the instructions for Israel to construct a tabernacle, a place for God to dwell with his people. The way the tabernacle is set up extensively mirrors the Garden of Eden.[4]

As mentioned above, the verbs used to describe the duties

of the priests in the tabernacle are the same as those used to describe the duties of Adam and Eve in the garden. Two golden cherubim are forged and placed on the ark of the covenant to guard it (Exodus 25:18-22), pointing back to the presence of an angel guarding the entrance to God's initial temple and place of dwelling in the Garden of Eden. The lampstand in the tabernacle, with flowers coming from seven branches seems to reflect a tree, possibly even the tree of life (Exodus 25:31-36). The gold of the tabernacle points back to the location of the Garden of Eden in a place where gold is prevalent (Exodus 25:11-39; Genesis 2:11-12). The entrance to the tabernacle faces east, just like the entrance to the Garden of Eden (Numbers 3:38; Genesis 3:23-24). When God's glory filled the tabernacle in Exodus 40:34-38, it signified the partial recreation of the Garden of Eden and a part of God's plan for making his dwelling place with his people once again.

Development

In Numbers 22-24, the theme of Israel as God's Tabernacle occurs in several places. First, as Balaam is journeying to meet Balak, he is stopped by an angel with a sword (22:31). Balaam is coming from the east, as seen in his statement in 23:7 where he says that "Balak brought me from Aram, the king of Moab from the eastern mountains." The presence of an angel with a sword barring the way of someone approaching from the east reminds the reader of the angel stationed outside of the Garden of Eden in Genesis 3:23-24. Thus from the context of this story, Israel is held up as a parallel to the Garden of Eden, guarded by a sword-wielding messenger of God.

Balak brings Balaam to high places where he can see the nation of Israel laid out before him (Numbers 22:41; 23:13-14; 24:2). As he overviews the nation encamped around the tabernacle (detailed in Numbers 2-3), Balaam gives a unique description to the nation. First, he notices that God is among them (23:21). The presence of the glory of God in the midst of Israel is unmistakable, even to a pagan diviner.

However, Balaam's words in 24:5-7 carry more importance to the discussion at hand. He says, "How beautiful are your tents, Jacob, your dwelling places, Israel! Like valleys they spread out, like gardens beside a river, like aloes planted by the LORD, like cedars beside the waters. Water will flow from their buckets; their seed will have abundant water." Balaam equates Israel with a garden planted beside a river, just like the Garden of Eden that had a river flowing from it (Genesis 2:10-14). Balaam recognizes that Israel is situated like the Garden of Eden as he describes the peoples' tents as trees and plants growing near the water.

Interestingly, the Hebrew word in verse 6 meaning "aloes" is different in the Septuagint, the Greek translation of the Old Testament. In the Greek, the word is "tents" or "tabernacles." This interpretive translation places the notion of the tabernacle together with the imagery of the Garden of Eden and applies both to the nation of Israel.[5] If 24:6 is taken as "like tabernacles planted by the LORD," Balaam is saying that Israel is a garden/tabernacle, the place of God's dwelling with his people whom he is using to bring his glory to the ends of the earth. This is further evidenced by verse 7, which speaks of water overflowing from Israel's buckets and Israel's seed increasing in the water. This shows God's desire to increase the size of his people as he desired to increase the size of the Garden of Eden. Numbers 22-24 portrays Israel as a recreated Garden of Eden for God's dwelling and expansion of glory.

Post-Numbers Expansion

The theme of God's presence with his people in a recreated Garden of Eden continues after Balaam's oracles. As the nation of Israel prepares to enter the land of Canaan, an angel with a drawn sword appears to Joshua in Joshua 5:13-15. As the nation of Israel approaches the promised land from the east, having just crossed the Jordan river in chapter 3, they are met by an angel barring their way. After Balaam speaks of Israel using garden and tabernacle imagery, Joshua 5 presents the land into which they enter the same way as the Garden of Eden was described in Genesis 3. The next step in recreating God's dwelling place in the nation of Israel is bringing them into their land.

Once Israel is securely in the land, Solomon sets out to create a permanent dwelling place for the Lord by building a temple (1 Kings 6:1). The temple bears the same marks of resemblance to the Garden of Eden as does the tabernacle, but this time larger, grander, and more permanent. At the dedication of the temple, Israel's priests bring in the ark of the covenant to the inner most part of the temple and, as they leave, the presence of the Lord descends mightily upon the temple (1 Kings 8:6-11). Solomon sees this and poignantly says, "The LORD has said that he would dwell in a dark cloud; I have indeed built a magnificent temple for you, a place for you to dwell forever" (8:12-13).

However, God does not dwell in this building forever. Ezekiel 8-9 describes the idolatry present in the temple and God's displeasure with it. These descriptions are followed in chapter 10 by Ezekiel seeing the glory of the Lord rise from its place in the inner room. God's glory is accompanied by cherubim and travels first into the threshold of the temple and then out of the temple entirely (10:3-18). The rebellion and idolatry that cast Israel into exile result in God leaving the temple, much like Adam and Eve's sin resulted in their exile and removal from God's presence.

But this is not the last Ezekiel has to say on the matter. In chapter 37 he sees a valley of dry bones into which God breathes new life by means of his Spirit (37:1-14). Directly following this, God tells him that he will bring back his people into their own land and make them one nation (37:20-22). They will be his people, and he will be their God (37:23). God's work in enlivening the people by means of his Spirit is confirmed in the everlasting covenant of peace he will make with Israel (37:26). All of this results in God saying, "My dwelling place will be with them; I will be their God and they will be my people. Then the nations will know that I the Lord make Israel holy, when my sanctuary is among them forever" (37:27-28). God promises to bring the people back into their land and dwell amongst them once again, this time forever. God also gives Ezekiel a detailed vision of a temple in 40-48 that is descriptive of God's future dwelling with his people.

God's dwelling has moved from the Garden of Eden to the Tabernacle and then to the Temple. In the face of God leaving the temple as a result of Israel's sin, Ezekiel promises an even greater dwelling of God with his people. And the fulfillment of God's intention to dwell with his people comes in the person of Jesus Christ.

John 1:14 says, "And the Word became flesh and made his dwelling among us. We have seen his glory, the glory of the one and only Son, who came from the Father, full of grace of truth." When John says that the Word, Jesus, dwelt among humans, he uses the Greek verb with the same root as the word used in Numbers 24:6 to describe Israel as tabernacles. Jesus, as God and man, brings the dwelling place and glory of God to the midst of humans. The entrance of this temple into the world is also marked by angels, as Mary, Joseph and the magi are all contacted by God's messengers in accordance with Christ's birth (Luke 1:26-38; Matthew 1:20-23; 2:19-20; 2:12)

This truth is seen even more explicitly in John 2:13-22, which records a story of Jesus in the temple. During the story, Jesus declares that if the temple was destroyed, he could rebuild it in three days (2:19). John adds an inspired note that "the temple he had spoken of was his body" (2:21). Jesus himself is the temple, the place where God's glory resides among his people. The second Adam would not fail where the first one did, but instead would rightly established God's temple on earth.

After the temple of Jesus' body was rebuilt following his death, Jesus ascended into heaven and God's presence and glory seemingly left his people once again. But Jesus had promised that when he left he would send them the Spirit of Truth to be with them (John 14:16-17). This enables Paul to say in 1 Corinthians 3:16 that believers are God's temple since the Spirit resides in them. In chapter 6 he adds, "Do you not know that your bodies are temples of the Holy Spirit, who is in you, whom you have received from God? ... Therefore, honor God with your bodies" (6:19-20). The Spirit resides corporately and individually in the church, making God's dwelling literally in his people. No longer does his presence dwell in a physical building; through the work of the Spirit, as prophesied in Ezekiel 37, God now dwells in his people, his temple. As Israel was spoken of as the Garden of Eden and the tabernacle, so the church becomes the temple of God.

And yet an even greater reality awaits. John sees a vision of the final restoration between God and man in Revelation 21-22. He says in 21:2-3, "I saw the Holy City, the new Jerusalem, coming down out of heaven from God, prepared as a bride beautifully dressed for her husband. And I heard a loud voice from the throne saying, 'Look! God's dwelling place is now among the people, and he will dwell with them. They will be his people, and

God himself will be with them and be their God.' " He adds in 21:22-23, "I did not see a temple in the city, because the Lord God Almighty and the Lamb are its temple. The city does not need the sun or the moon to shine on it, for the glory of God gives it light, and the Lamb is its lamp."

Beale says, "the temple of God has been transformed into God, his people and the rest of the new creation as the temple."[6] In 22:1-5, John describes this eternal temple using language reminiscent of the Garden of Eden, further proving this conclusion. The final unification of the triune God with his people in eternal paradise acts as the culmination of God's glory being made known over the entire world.

Conclusion

Though Adam failed to fulfill his role as vice-regent, priest, and image-bearer in God's original temple, God did not give up on his people. Numbers 24 contains an important passage that shows that God is recreating Israel as his temple. It zeroes in by showing that God still desires to dwell with his people. It zooms out by describing Israel already as God's dwelling and pointing forward to God's greater plan to make them into his dwelling. The shaping of God's people as his dwelling place comes into play as the nation's idolatry forces God to leave the temple in Ezekiel 10. At that point God does not abandon the nation altogether, but rather reveals that he desires to regenerate his dead people and dwell among them (Ezekiel 37).

This becomes a reality through the work of Jesus, the better Adam and better temple, who brings the glory of God among the people. When Jesus physically leaves earth he leaves behind his Spirit who furthers God's temple on earth by enlarging the church. The theme of the temple and God dwelling with his people culminates in Revelation, where John sees the eternal state of God and man together in a cosmic temple.

Michael Dietzel

Chapter 8

In the Latter Days

The theme that ties together the three previous themes is that of the temporal marker "in the latter days" (sometimes translated "in days to come" or "in the last days," though the phrase in the Hebrew and Greek is the same). The latter days are only mentioned once in Numbers 22-24 (24:14), but the significance of this one occurrence is high. The phrase is mentioned several times explicitly and a few more times implicitly in the Old Testament and is also expounded upon in the New Testament.

This temporal marker does not function in the same way as the other three themes, but rather shows how they are connected. It serves as a marker that explains how the information around it should be treated. The latter days is a temporal marker because it designates that the context of the events it delineates have a different time than the material around it. It is a marker because it signals special attention, and it is a temporal marker because it signals a specific time. A temporal maker draws the attention of the reader and needs different treatment than the unmarked material surrounding it.

Think about sports fans gathering to watch a baseball game between the Kansas City Royals and the Chicago Cubs in a bar near Wrigley Field. Since the baseball game is in Chicago, it would be assumed that the patrons who entered the bar would be Cubs fans, but those who are rooting for the Royals would mark themselves off by wearing a hat or shirt with the team logo. This would also result in different treatment for those marked off as Kansas City fans than for the Cubs fans. In the same way, passages marked off as taking place in the latter days should be treated differently, as they point beyond the present context to a deeper reality.

Beale has persuasively argued both that Adam and Eve were supposed to tend the Garden of Eden and consummate God's intentions for the world and humanity, and that after they sinned, the same pattern was followed by other characters of Scripture with the same goal.[1] He considers this to be an eschatological enterprise as the participants all seek to consummate the plan already inaugurated by God.

Beale shows that the idea of the latter days plays a large role in this eschatological endeavor. However, he argues that it "refers not to the future in general but rather to the final outcome of future events."[2] "The latter days" marks the material around it as referring to God's plan to consummate the new creation and bring humanity back into a right relationship with him. As with Royals fans in a Chicago bar, passages stamped with "the latter days" should be treated differently than the material around them.

Context

The phrase "in the latter days" occurs only once before Numbers 22-24. Jacob begins the blessing of his sons in Genesis 49:1 by saying, "Gather around so I can tell you what will happen to you in days to come." Genesis 49 has already been mentioned because of other themes it carries, specifically Judah described as a lion who conquers his enemies, the scepter of Judah that will not depart until the obedience of the nations comes to him, and the blessing attributed to Joseph in terms of a new creation. These themes are important in and of themselves, but they carry even greater theological freight because Jacob says they will occur in the latter days.

In the blessings Jacob gives to his children, the themes of new creation and restoration come to the foreground. The blessings given to Judah regarding his future reign and rule indicate that power, authority, and dominion will come to him, qualities similar to those Adam had in the Garden of Eden. The language used to describe Judah's reign also points back to the Garden: "He will tether his donkey to a vine, his colt to the choicest branch; he will wash his garments in wine, his robes in the blood of grapes. His eyes will be darker than wine, his teeth whiter than milk" (Genesis 49:11-12). "Nature will be renewed so much that vines will serve as hitching-posts for donkeys, and wine will be used for washing clothes."[3] Also, as has been shown above, the language used in Joseph's blessing recalls the blessing God gave creation in Genesis 1:28 and points to an Edenic state. The fact that these descriptions occur in the context of the latter days shows that the latter days will be a time of fulfillment and consummation for God's plan.

Development

The next time the latter days show up after Genesis 49:1 is in the oracles of Balaam.[4] They are mentioned once in Numbers 22-24, serving as the introduction to Balaam's fourth oracle in 24:14. Before Balaam returns to his people, he delivers a final parting blow to Balak, prophesying about things that will happen in the eschatological state, which again does not necessarily refer to the distant future, but to the period of the consummation of God's plan for the new creation. This temporal marker differentiates the material in the fourth oracle from that of the previous three and expands the range of application.[5]

Balaam opens his fourth oracle much like he opens his

third, testifying to the clarity of vision and hearing he now has because of God's hand in opening his eyes and ears (Numbers 24:15-16; cf. 24:3-4). Balaam goes on to say that with his clear vision, he sees someone, though he is not near temporally or spatially (24:17). The one he sees is the already discussed star from Jacob and scepter from Israel who will crush the head of Moab and the skulls of the people of Sheth. Numbers 24:18-24 describes the reign of this star and scepter, mentioning Edom, Seir, Amalek, the Kenites, Ashur, and Eber as enemies whom the future king will conquer. The multitude of nations shows how pervasive this king's reign will be; his kingdom will not just extend to the borders of Israel's promised land, but to the ends of the earth.

Balaam explicitly mentions the star of Jacob, the scepter of Israel, and the crushing of the heads of God's enemies in relationship to the latter days, but the themes he mentioned previously also relate indirectly to the temporal marker. The latter days serves as an explanation for how the Abrahamic blessing (and, by implication, cursing) woven throughout Balaam's oracles would be ultimately fulfilled. It shows how the lion of Judah will come and conquer his enemies. It gives the context for the recreation of the Garden of Eden as God's temple and dwelling place with his people. The implications of these explanations will be explored below.

Post-Numbers Expansion

The first mention of the latter days after Numbers 24 occurs in Deuteronomy 4:30. Here Moses tells the people that when they commit idolatry and are cast out of the land, they will return to the Lord and obey him in the latter days.[6] The reason for this is that the Lord is merciful and will not forget the covenant he made with their ancestors (Deuteronomy 4:31). Moses also mentions the latter days in Deuteronomy 31:29, focusing more on the destruction and exile that will come upon the people of Israel in that time: "In days to come, disaster will fall on you because you will do evil in the sight of the LORD and arouse his anger by what your hands have made." This exile spoken of in Deuteronomy 4:30 and 31:29 are eschatological realities because of the link with the latter days.[7] The return from exile is also in view, as Dempster links these passages with Numbers 24 in reference to the Abrahamic blessing that will be poured out on God's people.[8]

In Joshua 24:27, Joshua explains that a stone will be a witness against the people if they enter into disobedience. Though not present in the Hebrew text, the Septuagint adds the phrase, "And this shall be among you for a witness in the latter days, at the time when you deal falsely with the Lord my God." This seems to be a direct link to the two passages from Deuteronomy that speak about the exile of God's people in the latter days.[9]

Isaiah 2:2 serves as an extremely important passage which

references the latter days. In those days, Isaiah says, "the mountain of the LORD's temple will be established as the highest of the mountains; it will be exalted above the hills, and all nations will stream to it." Beale says, "Isa. 2:2 appears to be developing Gen. 49:1, 10, where at the eschatological zenith of the "latter days" "the obedience of the peoples..." will be given to the king of Israel."[10] The focus of this passage in Isaiah 2 is the peaceful time that will occur when the nations of the earth submit themselves to the Lord at his mountain temple. This relates to the scepter from Judah referenced in Genesis 49:10 and Numbers 24:17 and imagery of the garden temple as a mountain in Numbers 24:5-7, as well as connecting to the return from the exile spoken of in Deuteronomy 4:30.

Micah 4:1-5 mirrors Isaiah 2:2-5.[11] Micah, however, includes more imagery of the new creation, speaking about vines and fig trees in 4:4 that remind the reader of Jacob's blessings to Judah and Joseph in Genesis 49:11-12 and 22 respectively.[12]

Hosea 3:4-5 mentions a return from exile, the reign of a Davidic king, and blessings from the Lord in relation to the latter days. Verse 5 says "Afterward the Israelites will return and seek the LORD their God and David their king. They will come trembling to the LORD and to his blessings in the last days." As has been mentioned above, Hosea points to the return of Davidic king who will lead Israel out of exile. Hosea adds to the idea of return from exile in Deuteronomy 4:30, explicitly referencing that verse in a way no other Old Testament passage does.[13]

Michael Dietzel

Jeremiah references the latter days four times. He says in 23:20, "the anger of the LORD will not turn back until he fully accomplishes the purposes of his heart. In days to come you will understand it clearly." This testifies that Israel may not understand the reason or necessity of their exile until the eschatological time of fulfillment. He mentions the latter days with strikingly similar language in 30:24: "The fierce anger of the LORD will not turn back until he fully accomplishes the purposes of his heart. In days to come you will understand this." Beale adds, "The "latter days" of 30:24 are equivalent to "at that time" (31:1), "the days are coming" (31:27, 31, 38), "in those days" (31:29), and "after those days" (31:33), all of which designate the end-time of restoration."[14] Within this context, Jeremiah 31:31 specifically stands out: "'The days are coming,' declares the LORD, 'when I will make a new covenant with the people of Israel and with the people of Judah.'" This covenant will place the law of God in the hearts and minds of God's people (31:33) and all will know the Lord (31:34).

The next reference to the latter days in Jeremiah comes in relationship to Moab, not Israel. After forty-six verses of cursing language aimed at Moab, 48:47 reads, "Yet I will restore the fortunes of Moab in days to come." Especially intriguing are the links to Numbers 24, because Balaam prophesied that the star of Jacob and the scepter of Israel would crush the head of Moab, the nation Balak represented (24:17).[15] Jeremiah 48 seems to focus on the fulfillment of the defeat of Moab by Israel, yet the final verse

98

in the chapter speaks of their restoration in the latter days. The chapter introduces the idea that, like Israel, foreign nations will undergo a time of punishment for their disobedience before being reconciled to God in the latter days.

This idea is developed in Jeremiah 49:34-39, this time with the nation of Elam. As with Moab, the nation receives punishment for their opposition to God, but in 49:39 God adds, "Yet I will restore the fortunes of Elam in days to come." A similar reference is made to the nation of Ammon in 49:6, though "the latter days" is replaced by a related temporal marker, "afterward." These references, along with the two previous passages in Jeremiah, point to a time when the nations will come into a peaceful existence with God at a time of new creation, just like other sections such as Genesis 49 and Isaiah 2.[16]

Ezekiel 38:16 references an enemy named Gog whom God brings against Israel in the latter days. God will do this "so that the nations may know me when I am proved holy through you before their eyes." This refers primarily to a time of tribulation that Israel will go through as has been seen in previous references. This verse is interesting, however, because of the reference to Gog and the potential connection between this enemy and Agag mentioned in Numbers 24:7, a king whom the lion of Judah will conquer. The Septuagint translates Agag as Gog in 24:7, further enforcing this possible connection.[17] Though David conquered Agag's Amalekites in 1 Samuel 15:33, a greater Davidic king will conquer Gog in the latter days.[18]

The last references to the latter days in the Old Testament in Daniel. The first comes in chapter 2 when Daniel is interpreting king Nebuchadnezzar's dream of the statue and the stone. Daniel tells the king that God "has shown King Nebuchadnezzar what will happen in days to come." He then explains that the statue represents different human kingdoms that will be ultimately destroyed and replaced by a kingdom of God, not cut by human hands, that will grow and fill the entire earth, enduring forever (Daniel 2:35, 44). The image of a mountain representing the kingdom of God immediately draws to mind Isaiah 2 and Micah 4 and gives another picture of what will happen in the latter days.[19]

In Daniel 10:14, an angel comes to Daniel and tells him, "Now I have come to explain to you what will happen to your people in the future, for the vision concerns a time yet to come." This focuses on the tribulation Israel will undergo in the future which has been discussed in Daniel 7-8 and will be explained further by the angel in 11-12. This latter section of Daniel includes another link to Numbers 24, as 11:30 mentions the ships of Kittim that will come against an enemy king, ships mentioned in Numbers 24:24 which will afflict Asshur and Eber. This shows that the defeat of God's enemies foretold to take place in the latter days in Numbers 24 is the same defeat of God's enemies prophesied in Daniel 10.[20] Another important piece of information that will occur in the latter days is the resurrection of the dead, spoken about in Daniel 12:2-3.

The New Testament contains several references to the latter days, though the terminology used as the temporal marker is not always exactly the same. Though they are not exactly the same, the fact that they all point to a distinct temporal period different than the context surrounding them indicates that we should treat them in the same vein as the latter days language of the Old Testament.

Phrases like "the end of the age," "in the age to come," or "forever," point to the final judgment (Matthew 13:39-40, 49), Christ's everlasting presence with his people (Matthew 28:20), eternal life (Mark 10:30; Luke 18:30), and resurrection from the dead (Luke 20:34-35).[21] The apostle John uses latter day terminology frequently, focusing on the final judgment of unbelievers and bodily resurrection of believers.[22] There are also links between John and Daniel in reference to an hour coming when the dead will rise again. John 5:25 says "Very truly I tell you, a time (hour) is coming and has now come when the dead will hear the voice of the Son of God and those who hear will live" (Cf. Daniel 12:1-2; John 5:28-29). The eternal life promised to occur in the latter days in Daniel has come in the person of Jesus, for he says "whoever hears my word and believes him who sent me has eternal life and will not be judged but has crossed over from death to life" (John 5:24).[23]

Later in John, Jesus references this hour again, telling his Father, "The hour has come. Glorify your Son, that your Son may glorify you." This hour points to the cross, the pinnacle of Jesus' ministry on earth and the means God uses to bring about the new creation and bring his people back into relationship with him. 2 Corinthians 5:17 says, "Therefore if anyone is in Christ, the new creation has come: The old has gone, the new is here!" In reference to its use in the Old Testament, the New Testament uses latter day terminology to say that the latter days find inaugurated fulfillment in Christ's first coming.

Another important reference to the latter days in John comes in chapter 4, when Jesus tells the Samaritan woman at the well that "a time is coming and has now come when the true worshipers will worship the Father in the Spirit and in truth, for they are the kind of true worshipers the Father seeks" (John 4:23). Part of the latter days involves the presence of the Spirit of God in the worship of believers.

This finds further backing in Acts 2:17, when Peter quotes Joel to have said, "In the last days, God says, I will pour out my Spirit on all people." Joel 2:28 does not say "in the last days" but rather "afterward," but these terms are elsewhere treated as parallel and interchangeable (Hosea 3:5).[24] Peter's application of this text from Joel to the events of Pentecost show that the latter days which began in Jesus are continued in his representative body on earth, the church, through the work of his Spirit. Beale says, "The resurrection marked the beginning of Jesus' messianic reign, and the Spirit at Pentecost signaled the inauguration of his rule through the church (see Acts 1:6-8; 2:1-43).[25]

Two other significant references in the New Testament to

the latter days come in Paul's pastoral epistles. 1 Timothy 4:1-2 and 2 Timothy 3:1 both say that false teachers will come in the latter days, and the fact that the church in Ephesus was already experiencing false teaching shows that these latter days had already begun.[26]

Hebrews 1:2 contains perhaps the closest linguistic link to the Old Testament idea of the latter days. The author begins his letter by saying, "In the past God spoke to our ancestors through the prophets at many times and in various ways, but in these last days he has spoken to us by his Son, whom he appointed heir of all things, and through whom also he made the universe." God's Son, Jesus Christ, is the one who has revealed God in the latter days. Beale suggests that Hebrews 1:2 specifically alludes to Numbers 24 because it certainly alludes to Psalm 2 with regard to Jesus being established as the heir to all things and because Psalm 2 focuses on a ruling king with a scepter that will crush the nations.[27] Hebrews 1:2 indicates that the ministry of Jesus takes place in the latter days, confirming the testimony of the New Testament that the promises of the latter days have begun to be fulfilled in the work of Jesus Christ.

Conclusion and Synthesis

This discussion of the latter days provides the appropriate context to synthesize the material of Numbers 22-24 and describe the impact of the themes conveyed in Balaam's oracles to the greater storyline of Scripture. The greatest question that arises in the reading of these three chapters is whether or not God will bless disobedient Israel. At every step of the way, this question is answered as a resounding yes, and God shows that it is Balak and Moab, not Israel, who will be cursed for seeking to curse Israel. God remembers his covenant with Israel and he will not turn back on it.

In addition, Balaam speaks about a king who will come out of Israel and lead them, a lion from the tribe of Judah and a star and scepter who will crush the heads of his enemies. This king will have much greater power than Balak, the foreign king who will have his own head crushed for seeking to curse Israel. This king is viewed synonymously with the nation, and acts as a representative in terms of the Exodus and of having dominion over enemies. The prophecies about this king also hearken back to promises made to Abraham and Jacob and act as affirmations of them.

Balaam views the nation of Israel in terms of the Garden of Eden. The nation is like a renewed Eden and shows God's hand in recreating all things through his interaction with Israel. This is striking given the fact that Israel has been following in the footsteps of the failure of Adam and Eve rather than obeying and acting as a holy nation. Where Israel is faithless, God is faithful. God's presence with the people is also striking, as he shows that his desire is to dwell among them.

The reference to the latter days also connects Balaam's oracles with the promises of God to Israel, specifically the blessings given by Jacob to his children that show God's continued working in them. The latter days indicate a time when God will work restoration of creation, dominion, and blessing, and Balaam unites these themes under this temporal marker. This theme also shows that the culmination of blessing, a conquering king, and a renewed place of God dwelling with his people will not come immediately.

The history of the nation of Israel develops these themes. The blessing Adam and Eve had as God's people in the Garden of Eden was replaced by a curse. Now God begins to restore this blessing with his new people, Israel. God's blessing is seen in their dwelling in the land, conquering their enemies, and national growth in numbers and prosperity. However, these blessings are not final, as the nation rebels to the point of being exiled, equivalent to being cursed, and lose their God-given blessings. However, a time of future blessing is promised when the exile is over. God does not forget his promises.

The Edenic dominion evidenced by Adam and Eve's care in the garden begins to be restored in the nation of Israel. They receive a line of kings from the tribe of Judah, scepters who crush the head of their enemies and provide peace and blessing for the nation. However, these kings eventually lead the nation into destruction like Adam before them, and the nation goes into exile kingless. Nevertheless, God promises to establish an eternal reign through the descendants of David, and the nation holds on to this hope.

God dwells with his people in the tabernacle and then in the gloriously decorated temple. The model of the Garden of Eden shows signs of being restored as Israel seeks to obey God in their midst. However, the sin of the people increases to a point where God leaves the temple and ceases to dwell with his people. In the face of this, Israel is not hopeless, but clings to the fact that God still desires to dwell with his people and will provide a way to do so.

Israel looks forward to a future time when the right relationship between God and man, like it was in the Garden of Eden, can be restored. The latter days echo through Israel's history as a future time of glorious victory for Israel, even though they often resound off the walls of failure and defeat. With the promise of restoration comes the promise of judgment for sins. Israel goes into exile and then returns, showing that these latter days have begun, but their return from exile leaves much to be desired in terms of the glorious restoration promised throughout the prophets.

These themes all find fulfillment in the coming of Jesus Christ. Jesus acts as a representative and better Israel who brings blessing to all who believe in him. He is a Judaic king, born in the town of David, and marked out by a star. He tabernacles with his people and declares himself to be a better temple which he rebuilds in three days at his resurrection. He speaks freely of the final hour that has now come and tells his listeners that the blessings and glory that was prophesied about the latter days can be theirs if they only believe in him. As the Israelites returned from physical exile in partial fulfillment of the latter days, Jesus provides an escape from spiritual exile by conquering sin and relinquishing its grasp on people.

Numbers 22-24 directly links these themes to the person of Jesus. The blessing to Israel that God upholds is linked with the promise of a king from Judah and God's dwelling place with his people, all set in the context of the latter days. The greatest blessing the world has ever known comes in the salvation Jesus offers first to the Jews and then to the Gentiles, showing how God would bless all the nations of the earth through Abraham's descendants. The lion of Judah, the scepter of Israel, and the star of Jacob is none other than Jesus Christ, the one who also fulfills the prophecy of an eternal heir of the throne of David. The glorious imagery of a recreated Eden as God's dwelling place and temple points forward to God's physical dwelling with his people in the form of Jesus. Jesus' life on earth represents the beginnings of a new age, specifically the latter days, when themes like the three aforementioned find fulfillment.

However, Jesus' first coming is not the final consummation for these themes. While believers in Christ have the blessing of eternal life, and even share in this life now, they have not yet entered into the full extent of the spiritual and physical life they will have with Jesus for eternity. While Jesus reigns over his creation and his people, he has not yet defeated all his enemies fully. While Jesus dwelt on earth with his people and now dwells spiritually in every person who believes in him, he will dwell physically with his people for eternity as his dwelling place is once again with humanity. Though the latter days have begun in the life and work of Jesus, the peace and restoration promised to occur in that time have not yet come to pass. There is more to come.

The fact that these themes are all mentioned in Numbers 22-24 shows that these chapters are critically important to understand. They pick up themes introduced in Genesis 1-3, 12, 15, 17, and 49 which are critical to God's plan for the world. These themes are then referenced in places such as Deuteronomy 4, 27-28, and 31, 2 Samuel 7, Psalm 2 and 110, Isaiah 2, Jeremiah 24, 30, 32, and 48, Ezekiel 37 and 38, Hosea 3 and 11, Micah 4 and 5, Matthew 2, Luke 4, John 1, 4, Acts 2, Galatians 3, Hebrews 1, and Revelation 21 and 22. The oracles of Balaam provide an important development in God's plan for the world, and as such must be studied and understood along with other important passages.

One of the intriguing aspects of the biblical theological developments in Numbers 22-24 is their context in the story of the Pentateuch. As has been mentioned above, Numbers showcases Israel's disobedience, and the careful reader should expect God to curse his people through Balak and Balaam who desire to curse. The political and spiritual powers of earth align against Israel, and God is presented with a perfect opportunity to carry out righteous wrath against his people. However, the promises which are mentioned and developed in these chapters show emphatically that God will not abandon his plan and that it will be even more glorious than previously expected.

For the original audience of the nation of Israel and the modern audience of the church, the biblical theological truths contained in Numbers 22-24 provide deep encouragement and warrant careful study because of the vast impact they have on a person's view of God's work in their lives.

Michael Dietzel

Conclusion

We have come a long way since the beginning of our journey.
We started by introducing biblical theology and its focus on discovering
the interpretive methods of the authors and the themes they employ
and develop. We then used biblical theology to study Numbers 22-24,
mining four truths from the themes that Moses, the later editor,
Balaam, and God take from the previous Pentateuchal texts and mold
together in these three chapters. We also looked forward to the rest of
Scripture to see how the later authors of Scripture did the same with
these four themes.

As I stated in the preface, studying these themes serves three
purposes, the first two specifically and the third a result of the first
two. I hope those who read this will use this introduction to biblical
theology to begin to do it in other parts of Scripture. Now that you have
read Numbers 22-24 (hopefully on your own and not just through my
synopsis) and one author's attempt to flesh out its developments and

connections, you can use the tools you have picked up to read the rest of Scripture through the lens of biblical theology. I would recommend starting at the beginning, all the way back to Genesis, and reading the entire story of Scripture over and over again. As you read, look for the themes of Scripture that are repeated multiple times and developed in different ways. Look for the things that the author tries to emphasize and place them at the forefront of your mind as well. This focus on how the author intentionally shapes the story, whether in a few chapters or the storyline of Scripture as a whole, will help you understand God's Word more clearly.

The second purpose for this work is that the specific themes might impact readers as well. In the Balaam narrative, God shows extravagantly that he will bless his people regardless of whether they deserve it. The odds can be stacked against his blessed ones to the highest degree, but he will never renege on his promise. God overcomes human powers by means of a more powerful lion-king, who we know to be Jesus. Our king rules even now and conquers those who oppose his children. God continues to emphasize dwelling with his people, and the church today embodies that dwelling as the Spirit dwells within us. Oh the never ending extent of God's faithfulness to and love for his people! In addition, Balaam's reference to things he sees that will happen in the latter days reminds us to make the most of the time, as we live in those latter days today. God is keeping his promises, and now we must respond by pursuing him in obedience.

These themes are worth dwelling on further than a couple dozen pages here. In my study towards this work I can testify to the effect they have had on me personally. I could go on and on (and someday I'm sure I will in a solid sermon series) regarding the implications and encouragements that can be gained from these four themes. More time in the text will lead to greater blessings for you as well. I encourage you to do so.

The general doing of biblical theology and the specific implications of the themes found in this study of biblical theology lead to the third purpose of the book, magnifying Jesus Christ in his work of salvation. If biblical theology follows the story of Scripture, it makes sense that it focuses on its main character. And by applying biblical theology to this text we can see how even from the mouth of a pagan magician thousands of years before Christ's entry into the world, God was accomplishing his plan to redeem the world.

Thanks for joining me on this journey. I God grows you through his truth in Numbers 22-24 and in his truth you will read in the rest of Scripture as you do biblical theology yourself. Praise be to God for his faithfulness, his blessing, his reign, his immanence, and his salvation

About the Author

Michael Dietzel lives in Overland Park, Kansas, and enjoys books, Taylor Swift, Charlie Brown, and the Kansas City Royals. He contributed to the *Encyclopedia of Christianity in the United States* (Rowman and Littlefield, 2016). He has a BA in Biblical Languages and an MA in Biblical Studies from Northland International University. He is currently serving among God's people at Countryside Baptist Church. He hopes to be a part of training the next generation of servant leaders for Great Commission living.

Michael Dietzel

Endnotes

Preface

[1] James M. Hamilton, *With the Clouds of Heaven*, NSBT (Downers Grove, IL: InterVarsity Press, 2014).

[2] Michael Summers Jr., *Surrender: A Christian's Guide to Dependence* (2016).

Chapter 1

[1] Hamilton, *With the Clouds of Heaven*, 21.

[2] Stephen Dempster, *Dominion and Dynasty* NSBT (Downers Grove, IL: InterVarsity Press, 2003), 15

Chapter 2

[1] The information in the previous two paragraphs are taken largely from Tremper Longman III and Raymond B. Dillard, *An Introduction to the Old Testament* 2nd ed. (Grand Rapids, Michigan: Zondervan, 2006), 41.

[2] Ibid.; Roland Kenneth Harrison, *Introduction to the Old Testament* (Grand Rapids, MI: Wm. B Eerdmans Publishing Company 1969), 497.

[3] Julius Wellhausen, *Prolegomena zur Geschichte Israels* (Berlin: Druck und verlag von G. Reimer, 1899). This theory was titled the Document Hypothesis or the JEDP theory. J represented the author who employed the term Yahweh, E the author who used Elohim, D the author of the Deuteronomic material, and P the author of the priestly content.

[4] John Sailhamer, *The Meaning of the Pentateuch* (Downers Grove, IL: IVP Academic, 2009).

[5] Ibid., 34.

[6] Table taken from a synthesis of Ibid., 33-36

[7] Ibid., 325, 37, 49. Sailhamer explains the marks of a second hand in compiling these poems in 325-332 and 337-340.

[8] Though the Spirit is not specifically mentioned in the fourth oracle, the fact that Balaam uses similar terminology in 24:15-16 as he does in 24:3-4 to describe the clarity of his senses and the fact that these words are from the Lord indicate that the Spirit is still speaking through him.

Chapter 3

[9] Jacob Milgrom, *Numbers*, The JPS Torah Commentary (Philadelphia: The Jewish Publication Society, 1990), 468; Dennis R. Cole, *Numbers*, NAC (Nashville: Holman Reference, 2000), 366; C. F. Keil, and F. Delitzsch, *Pentateuch*, trans. James Martin (Peabody, MA: Hendrickson Publishers, 2006), 761; Leander E. Keck, *Numbers, Deuteronomy, Introduction to Narrative Literature, Joshua, Judges, Ruth, 1 & 2 Samuel*, NIB (Nasvhille: Abingdon Press, 1998), 178. However, Ronald B. Allen, *Numbers*, in *Genesis, Exodus, Leviticus, Numbers*, ed. Frank E. Gaebelein, EBC, 12 vols. (Grand Rapids, MI: Zondervan, 1990), 888 says that Balaam was a sorcerer who sought to manipulate God.

[10] Milgrom, *Numbers*, 472.

[11] Cole, *Numbers*, 367; Milgrom, *Numbers*, 472; David L. Stubbs, *Numbers*, BTCB (Grand Rapids, MI: Brazos Press, 2009), 172.

[12] Stubbs, *Numbers*, 184-85; Origen, *Homilies on Numbers*, ed. L. Doutreleau SJ, *Origene, Homilies sur les Nombres*, SC 415, 442, 461 (Paris: Editions du Cerf, 1996-2001), 2.277.

[13] Negative Rabbinical texts: Philo, *On the Life of Moses 1*, 285-286; Josephus, *Antiquities*, 5.119-122; *b. Sanhedrin* XI.1.D, XI.2.C, XI.8.I-J, XI.9.K, XI.8.D. Positive Rabbinical texts: *Sifre* 26.142; *Numbers Rabbah* 14:20.

14 Stubbs, *Numbers*, 187.

Chapter 4

1 5:1-32 begins with Adam and ends with Noah, introducing the main character of the next three chapters. 10:1-32 begins with Noah and ends with Shem, the obedient son Noah had blessed in 9:26-27 and who would figure into the next phase of the narrative. 11:10-32 begins with Shem and settles on Terah and his family in verse 26, though with the mention of his death, his son Abram comes to the forefront. Abraham is the main character until his death in chapter 25, and even after his death he plays an important role in the Pentateuch and the rest of Scripture. See also 4:1-2 and 4:17-24 which, though not full genealogies, detail the births of Cain, Abel, and Seth and serve the same purpose as the genealogies do.

2 Dempster, *Dominion and Dynasty*, 77.

3 The only land Abraham ever owned in Canaan was a tomb in Machpelah near Mamre (Genesis 23:16) in which he buried Sarah, his wife (23:19) and in which Abraham himself (25:9), Isaac (35:28), and Jacob (50:13) were buried. Ironically, the first fruits of God's promise of land come through the emblem of death.

4 The following summary of the content of Numbers owes much to Ibid., 110-113. The material presented there is developed here.

5 Cf. Genesis 12:2; 13:16; 15:5; 17:4-6, 16; 22:17.

6 Ibid., 110.

7 Cf. Thomas Schreiner, The King in His Beauty (Grand Rapids, MI: Baker Academic, 2013), 76, who discusses the dual emphases of blessing and cursing in the narrative.

8 The theme of Balaam's inability to go against what the Lord tells him is

mentioned fifteen times in these three chapters: 22:8, 12-13, 18, 20, 35, 38; 23:3-5, 8, 12, 16, 20, 23, 26, 24:1-4, 12-16).

[9] Cf. Alter, The Art of Biblical Narrative, 104-07.

[10] One would think that this would grab Balaam's attention, but he treats it like another day at the office. Cf. Ibid., 106.

[11] Waltke with Yu, *Old Testament Theology*, 137-38.

[12] Balaam would have made these sacrifices with the intention of pleasing the Lord and ensuring that God would work in the way Balaam desired. See Ashley, *The Book of Numbers*, 466; Gordon J. Wenham, *Numbers,* TOTC (Nottingham, England: IVP Academic, 2008), 173; Keil and Delitzsch, *Pentateuch*, 771; Levine, *Numbers 21-36*, 162; John Calvin, *Commentaries On the Four Last Books of Moses: Arranged in the Form of a Harmony,* trans. Charles William Bingham, vol. 3 (Edinburgh: Calvin Translation Society, 2010), 201-02; Baruch A. Levine and J.-M. de Tarragon, "Shapshu Cries Out in Heaven: Dealing with Snakebites at Ugarit." *Revue Bilique* 95 (1987): 202-214.

[13] The reference to dust specifically alludes to Genesis 13:16: "I will make your offspring like the dust of the earth, so that if anyone could count the dust, then your offspring could be counted." God also promises in Genesis 12:2 and 17:4-6 and 16 that Abraham's descendants will be a great nation, in 15:5 that they will be as many as the stars in the sky, and in 22:17 that they will be as many as the stars in the sky and the sand on the seashore.

[14] See chapter seven for the discussion of the word used in the Hebrew (aloes) and the Greek LXX (tabernacles).

[15] The previous biblical texts have been quoted from the NIV, but the discussion of 24:7-9 draws from the ESV because this writer thinks it better represents the meaning of the text. See the discussion of the King from Judah in chapter six for further explanation.

[16] Genesis 49:1; Numbers 24:14; Deuteronomy 4:30; 31:29; Isaiah 2:2; Jeremiah 23:20; 30:24; 48:47; 49:39; Ezekiel 38:16; Hosea 3:5; Micah 4:1; Daniel 2:28; 10:14. Dempster, *Dominion and Dynasty*, 90; Ibid., fn. 50. See the discussion of the latter days in chapter eight for further explanation.

[17] A verse that comes in the context of the latter days (Genesis 49:1).

[18] The reference to Sheth (or Seth) is confusing, but given the parallelism evident in this oracle (and the other three as well) Sheth probably renames Moab. Cole, *Numbers*, 427, referencing Ashley, *The Book of Numbers*, 501, says, "...the phrase "children of Seth" would be the equivalent of the phrase "of Moab," hence described as one of the people groups from the lineage of Seth." Milgrom, *Numbers*, 210, identifies the children of Sheth/Seth with the Shutu, a tribal, nomadic people over whom Israel was promised dominion (Genesis 27:29).

[19] The reference to Seir in verse 18 (Seir, his enemy, will be conquered) is not a reference to another nation, but works like the parallelism between Moab and Sheth/Seth. Mt Seir was a prominent geographical feature in Edom and could be used interchangeably with the nation. Wenham, *Numbers*, 180; Cole, *Numbers*, 427.

Chapter 5

[1] Cf. Ronald B. Allen, "The Theology of the Balaam Oracles." In Tradition & Testament: Essays in Honor of Charles Lee Feinberg, ed. John S. and Paul D. Feinberg (Chicago: Moody Press, 1981), 84-85.

[2] 22:4-13; 22:16-20; 23:11-12; 23:25-26; 23:27-24:1; 24:10-13.

[3] Dempster, *Dominion and Dynasty*, 77 fn. 40. Curse language is also used in 8:21, in which God mentions a previous curse: "The Lord smelled the pleasing aroma and said in his heart: 'Never again will I curse the ground because of humans, even though every inclination of the human heart is evil from childhood. And

never again will I destroy all living creatures, as I have done.' "

[4] Ibid.

[5] Blessing terminology occurs six times in the Hebrew (49:25-2649:26) and seven in the Greek. The only other time blessing language occurs in this chapter is in the summary statement of 49:28, where it occurs three times. In addition, words connoting fruitfulness and growth show up in 49:22. This is the only such occurrence in chapter 49.

[6] The name Judah likely has its roots in the Hebrew word for praise. At Judah's birth in 29:35, Rachel says, "This time I will praise the Lord." Joseph in Hebrew possibly comes from the Hebrew word meaning "I add to or increase." At Joseph's birth in 30:24, Rachel says, "May the Lord add to me another son." *Enhanced Brown-Driver-Briggs Hebrew and English Lexicon*, s.v. יְהוּדָה ;יָסַף.

[9] Ronald Allen, *The Theology of the Balaam Oracles: A Pagan Diviner and the Word of God* (ThD dissertation, Dallas Theological Seminary, 1973), 433-437. Allen draws a parallel between Numbers 22-24 and Deuteronomy 4:31-40, positing that the latter text is a commentary on the former as it occurs somewhat concurrently in the Israelite camp below Balak and Balaam. The fact that the latter days are mentioned in Numbers 24:14 and Deuteronomy 4:30 lends credibility to this theory. In Deuteronomy 4 God reveals that Israel is blessed because of his love for them, not for any intrinsic quality within themselves.

[8] See endnote 15 in chapter four as well as the discussion in chapter six for an explanation of the use of the ESV rather than the NIV here.

[9] Blessing language occurs fifty-two times in the Hebrew and fifty times in the Greek. Cursing language occurs forty-six times in the Hebrew and thirty-seven times in the Greek.

[10] Jesus had just been anointed by the Holy Spirit at his baptism in Luke 3:21-22.

Chapter 6

[1] Klyne Snodgrass, "The Use of the Old Testament in the New," in New Testament Criticism and Interpretation, ed. David Alan Black and David S. Dockery (Grand Rapids MI: Zondervan, 1991), 416.

[2] Keil and Delitzsch, *Pentateuch*, 780, agree with E. W. Hengstenberg (*Dissertations on the Genuineness of the Pentateuch*, vol. 2, trans. J. E. Ryland (Edinburg: John D. Lowe, 1847), 250; *The History of Balaam and his Prophecies*, trans. J. E. Ryland (Edinburg: Dundee, 1848), 458) in positing that Agag served as the general title for Amalekite kings, thus creating a greater connection between David's defeat of the Amalekites and Numbers 24:7. However this should not be taken as more than a supposition.

[3] God speaks with similar sentiment two other times in Jeremiah. In 24:7 he says, "I will give them a heart to know me, that I am the LORD. They will be my people, and I will be their God, for they will return to me with all their heart." In 32:38 he adds, "They will be my people, and I will be their God."

[4] Some consider these Magi the spiritual descendants of Balaam: Eusebius, *Demonstratio Evangelica*, 9.1; Thomas Schreiner, *New Testament Theology: Magnifying God in Christ* (Grand Rapids, MI: Baker Academic, 2008), 678 fn. 12; Origen *Homilies*, 13.7.

[5] An inscription containing references to the magician Balaam was found in the Transjordan region to the west of Israel and points to his identification beyond the Old Testament. Thus, when the Magi, the ideological descendants of Balaam, were encountered with the presence of the star, it is probable that their research in ancient prophecies concerning stars led them to Balaam's oracles. They would have been familiar with him and likely interpreted his reference to the star in connection to the cosmic events they beheld. Regarding the inscription, the initial monograph written about the discovery is J. Hoftijzer and G. van der Kooij, *Aramaic Texts from Deir 'Alla* (Leiden: E. J.

Brill, 1976). Hoftijzer and van der Kooij revisited their findings in *The Balaam Text from Deir 'Alla Reevaluated: Proceedings of the International Symposium Held at Leiden, 21-24 August, 1989* (Ledien: E. J. Brill, 1991). Also see Baruch Levine, "Review: The Deir 'Alla Plaster Inscriptions," Journal of the American Oriental Society 101, no. 2 (April-June, 1981); and Jo Ann Hackett, *The Balaam Text from Deir 'Alla*, Harvard Semitic Monographs 31 (Decatur, GA: Scholar's Press, 1984).

[6] For a treatment of different possible types of fulfillment of Hosea 11 in Matthew 2, see Robert L. Plummer, "Righteousness and Peace Kiss: The Reconciliation of Authorial Intent and Biblical Typology." SBJT 14.2 (2010): 54-61. Also see his discussion in *40 Questions About Interpreting the Bible* (Grand Rapids, MI: Kregel Publications, 2010), 205-07.

[7] This idea, known as sensus plenior (fuller meaning), can be seen in John A. Broadus, *Commentary on the Gospel of Matthew* (Philadelphia: American Baptist Publication Society, 1886), 23.

[8] Sailhamer, *The Meaning of the Pentateuch*, 331; 339-40; 476-78 argues that the switch from plural to singular shows the evidence of the second author of the Pentateuch in interpreting Moses' original recording of Balaam's oracle. This accords with Sailhamer's theory that Numbers 24 is one of three major poems contributed by the later author that duplicate and expand upon the material before them (Genesis 49; Deuteronomy 32-33). Ibid., 330.

Chapter 7

[1] G. K. Beale, *The Temple and the Church's Mission* NSBT (Downers Grove, IL: InterVarsity Press, 2004), 81-82.

[2] Ibid., 66-80.

[3] See Numbers 3:7-8; 8:25-26; 18:5-6; 1 Chronicles 23:32; Ezekiel 44:14. Ibid., 66-67.

---

[4] The following points of similarities are taken from Ibid., 67-75.

[5] Ibid., 125.

[6] Ibid., 393.

Chapter 8

[1] G. K. Beale, *A New Testament Biblical Theology: The Unfolding of the Old Testament in the New* (Grand Rapids, MI: Baker Academic, 2011), 29-91; Idem., *The Temple and the Church's Mission*, 81.

[2] Idem., *A New Testament Biblical Theology*, 98.

[3] Dempster, *Dominion and Dynasty*, 91.

[4] Beale notes five connections between Genesis 49 and Numbers 22-24: 1. Genesis 49:9 and Numbers 24:9 include almost identical phrases about lion imagery; 2. Genesis 49:10 and Numbers 24:17 both reference a scepter; 3. Genesis 49:1 and Numbers 24:14 mention that the following prophecies occur in the latter days; 4. Numbers 24:8 and Genesis 49 both refer to the nations as God's enemies who are to be defeated; 5. Genesis 49:11-12, 22, 25-26 and Numbers 24:5-9 both connect Israel's future conqueror and new creation imagery. *A New Testament Biblical Theology*, 99-100.

[5] Sailhamer, *The Meaning of the Pentateuch*, 332 sees the latter days as a link between Genesis 49, Numbers 24, and Deuteronomy 32-33 (the latter days introduces these chapters in 31:29). He posits that these chapters show the signs of a later author who appended them to significant narrative portions in order to apply the material of the narratives to a greater time.

[6] "Here "the latter days" includes both the distress that is to come upon Israel and its returning to God as a result of that distress." Beale, *A New Testament Biblical Theology*, 101.

[7] Ibid., 102.

[8] "A real possibility of restoration to the land for Israel can occur if Israel gets a new heart in exile and repents 'in the latter days' (Deut. 4:30; 30:1-6). This expression of return to the land for Israel clearly links up with Jacob's and Balaam's blessings on Israel in the distant future." Dempster, *Dominion and Dynasty*, 121; Cf. John H. Sailhamer, *Introduction to Old Testament Theology: A Canonical Approach* (Grand Rapids, MI: Zondervan, 1995).

[9] Beale, *A New Testament Biblical Theology*, 102.

[10] Ibid., 104.

[11] Dempster, *Dominion and Dynasty*, 185.

[12] Beale, *A New Testament Biblical Theology*, 105.

[13] Beale points out that "the combined Hebrew wording of "return to the LORD their [or your] God" + "in the latter days" occurs nowhere else in the OT except these two passages." Ibid., 103.

[14] Ibid., 106.

[15] There are several connections between Jeremiah 48 and Numbers 22-24: In Jeremiah 48:15 God is referred to as a king, cf. Numbers 23:21; In Jeremiah 48:17 Moab's mighty scepter is broken, cf. Numbers 24:17; Jeremiah 48:25 says that Moab's horn is cut off, cf. Numbers 23:22; 24:8; Jeremiah 48:45 mentions the burning of the foreheads of Moab and the skulls of the noisy boasters, cf. Numbers 24:17.

[16] Ibid., 107.

[17] W. Horbury. "The Messianic Associations of 'The Son of Man.'" *JTS* 36 (1985), 39.

[18] Stubbs, *Numbers*, 194.

[19] Beale even suggests that Daniel may have been influenced by the two prophets. Beale, *A New Testament Biblical Theology, 108.*

[20] Sailhamer, *The Meaning of the Pentateuch*, 339-341 ties the ships of Kittim with the table of nations in Genesis 10, where the Kittites, a maritime people, are mentioned as the descendants of Japheth (10:4). Genesis 9:27 says that Japheth will live in the tents of Shem. Sailhamer posits that the Medes and Greeks, listed as descendants of Japheth in Genesis 10:2, and the people of Kittim inhabit the tents of the descendants of Shem: Babylon, Assyria, and Eber (Assyria and Eber are listed in Genesis 10:21-22). He also posits that the second author of the Pentateuch added this reference to Kittim in order to tie Balaam's oracles to the table of nations and show that the events surrounding Balaam are in line with Genesis 9:27. This position is interesting and probably correct, but Sailhamer does not give great support for the connections he draws between the nations and their references in the table of nations.

[21] Beale, *A New Testament Biblical Theology*, 130.

[22] Ibid., 131.

[23] Ibid., 131-132.

[24] Ibid., 103.

[25] Ibid., 137.

[26] See 1 Timothy 1:3-4, 6-7, 19-20; 4:7; 5:13-15; 6:20-21; 2 Timothy 1:15; 2:16-19, 25-26; 3:2-9. Ibid., 141. 2 Peter 3:3 and Jude 18 also make known the fact that scoffers and ungodly people will show themselves in the last days.

[27] Ibid., 142. He backs this theory up by mentioning that 2 Peter 1:17-19 also contains links to Psalm 2:7 and Numbers 24:17.

Made in the USA
Lexington, KY
05 November 2016